The Ignorant Perfection
of
Ordinary People

SUNY Series in Constructive Postmodern Thought

David Ray Griffin, Editor

The Ignorant Perfection
of
Ordinary People

ROBERT INCHAUSTI

STATE UNIVERSITY OF NEW YORK PRESS

Published by
State University of New York Press, Albany

For information, address State University of New York
Press, State University Plaza, Albany, N.Y., 12246

Production by Dana Foote
Marketing by Dana E. Yanulavich

Library of Congress Cataloging Publication Data

Inchausti, Robert, 1952–
    The Ignorant Perfection of Ordinary People / Robert Inchausti.
        p. cm.—(SUNY Series in Constructive Postmodern Thought)
    Includes bibliographical references and index.
    ISBN 0–7914–0677–6 (alk. paper).—ISBN 0–7914–0678–4
(pbk. alk. paper)
    1. Religious biography. 2. Political activists—Biography.
3. Postmodern. 4. World politics—20th century. I. Title.
II. Series.
    BL72.I53   1991
291'.092—dc20   90-40941
                                                     CIP

For Linda Garcia
Comrade in Arms, Plebeian Postmodern

There is a light in this world—a healing spirit more powerful than any darkness we may encounter. We sometimes lose sight of this force when there is suffering, too much pain. And suddenly this spirit will emerge through the lives of ordinary people who hear a call and answer in extraordinary ways.

—*Preface* to Ann and Jeanette Petrie's film *Mother Teresa*

CONTENTS

ACKNOWLEDGMENTS

I would like to thank Gary Cooper, George Cotkin, Maurice Friedman, David Ray Griffin, Mary Giles, Alan Howell, and Donald Sturtevant for their comments on earlier versions of this book. And thanks to Joe DeRuosi for helping me with my computer.

INTRODUCTION

*We have been silent witnesses of evil deeds, we have
been drenched by many storms; we have learned
the arts of equivocation and pretence; experience
has made us suspicious of others and kept us from
being truthful and open; intolerable conflicts have
worn us down and even made us cynical. Are we
still of any use? What we shall need is not geniuses,
or cynics, or misanthropes, or clever tacticians, but
plain, honest, straightforward men. Will our
inward power of resistance be strong enough for us
to find our way back to simplicity and
straightforwardness?*

—DIETRICH BONHOEFFER[1]

As we move into the last decade of the twentieth century, it is
becoming increasingly evident that the most progressive and lasting
political innovations in this century have not come from the expected
sources: violent revolutionaries or avant-garde social theorists. Rather
they have come from the practical achievements of moralists and religious reformers: simple and straightforward people like Mahatma
Gandhi, Martin Luther King, Jr., Mother Teresa, and Lech Walesa—
people who by their work and their example have created new movements for social justice and, in some instances, new techniques for
obtaining it.

These reformers base their movements upon such preindustrial
values as personal integrity and transcendental obligation. But they do
not derive these values from any authoritarian absolutes; instead they
discover them in the clash of their own personal commitments and
cultural heritage with the proud antihumanisms of the age. They discover them in the survival strategies of the concentration camp prisoner, in the transformative dignity of the nonviolent soldier of truth,
and in the rough and ready pragmatism of Eastern European labor
representatives. Simply by seeking justice and affirming the personal-

ism implicit in their own traditions, these "ordinary people" not only articulate an everyday spirituality to guide and refine practical reason, but they live it.

Admittedly some contemporary philosophers such as Richard Rorty have already affirmed the value of traditional religious mythologies as ways of talking about our ultimate concerns, but what is unique about the thinker-activists considered here is that they live *inside* the ethical imperatives and symbology of those traditions. And so, while they reject the false credulity that asserts an absolute literal identity between their particular religious creeds and the will of God, they also reject the detachment of the secular pluralist philosopher as an evasion of the religious responsibility to live out the visionary aspirations of their creeds. Their value as public philosophers derives primarily from their honest witness to the difficulties inherent in practicing what they preach.

For these practical progressives, religions are not epistemological assertions so much as vehicles of the sublime, calls to transcend the givens of experience in order to realize certain exquisite possibilities. Given this operational orientation, metaphysics, as a name for the sublime redefinition of experience, need not be overcome. But as a mystifying agent of privilege, it might well be taken apart. That is to say, whenever ideas are used as weapons of privilege, they ought to be criticised—not merely via analysis—but through actual human dialogue, concrete personal sacrifice, and direct confrontation with those persons and institutions exploiting their false authority.

There is, in effect, a metaphysics of light and a metaphysics of darkness. The metaphysics of light is systematically antifascist in its advocacy of the sublime. The metaphysics of darkness is Blake's dreaded priesthood, the pharisaic assault upon human solidarity made in the name of some privileged truth, method, or idea. Premoderns and primitives, those whose epistemologies predate the theoretical self-consciousness born of Enlightenment figures such as Descartes, tend to conflate and confuse these two realms. Postmoderns and moderns, those who build upon the traditions of Enlightenment skepticism, seek to avoid both by escaping metaphysical thought altogether. Whereas the religious activists examined here constantly seek to distinguish between these two realms, in order to define an ethic. They are not interested in establishing or exposing the foundations of thought. Their main intellectual concern is with making moral distinctions and in discerning the practical imperatives those distinctions imply.

This focus upon discernment derives in part from their common recognition of the universal human paradox that we are all products of a history written in blood—a history that confronts everyone of us with specific moral obligations that are born of profound collective tragedies that transcend our personal lives—and that at the same time we are also free subjectivities born to transform those obligations through healing acts of love and service and to turn the ironies of fate into opportunities for self-creation and social reform.

Given this tension built into the very fabric of our identities, progress cannot be defined solely in terms of the quest to extend individual freedoms. It must also be understood as obtaining access to the sources of our own original cultures—knowing who we are, where we come from, where our responsibilities lie, and, consequently, where our authentic heroism resides. Those who don't study history are not so much condemned to repeat it as they are to live anonymously within it, ignorant of the repetitive and hence symbolic nature of their actions and, therefore, unconscious of the larger drama of their own lives; morally and metaphysically diminished, trivialized, and rendered irresponsible—cut off as it were, from the sources of their own dignity.

In the many contemporary movements for human rights out of which several of these figures have emerged (from Poland's Solidarity movement to the Native American and La Raza movements in the United States), we see the birth of a new form of traditionalism: a traditionalism that honors the old ways, not for their fascist energy or authoritarian solace, but for their revolutionary potential to throw off the yoke of an increasingly dehumanizing, mystifying, and amnesic modern world. These new traditionalisms make possible an heroic response to existence; that is to say, a response to existence that is willful, dramatic, creative, and historically engaged, a response that tries to honor both the dead and the as yet unborn.[2]

One of the premises of this book is that these new counter-modernisms are a corrective response to the failure of both positivism and liberalism to establish a valid universal history. The search for a single, unified story of human development, which has largely been abandoned by professional philosophers and scientists, has fallen by default to those engaged in the process of becoming human, to those struggling for their rights, their lost histories, their true selves. The stories of their struggles form an emerging ethic that constitutes at least a new world critique, if not a new world view.

Gustavo Gutierrez described these developments this way:

> The poor, the wretched of the earth, are not, in the first instance, questioning the religious world or its philosophical suppositions. They are calling into question first of all the

economic, social, and political order that oppresses and mar-
ginalizes them, and, of course, the ideology that is brought in
to justify this domination.[3]

But it is not only the poor who feel marginalized. This sense of
being reduced and robbed of one's essential self cuts across several
worlds of experience. There is a growing worldwide recognition that by
refusing to accept the intolerable and by acting on one's deepest con-
victions (sometimes even before one possesses any sure theoretical
justifications for them) one can acquire a fresh understanding of one's
place in history and with that new understanding discover hitherto
unimagined solidarities with other people. Suddenly what once may
have appeared to be a heterogeneous set of discrete outrages (economic
inequality, ecological crisis, alienation, starvation, traffic jams, poor
public education, and an increase in tasteless foods and entertain-
ments) now stands revealed as the systematic products of a global
modernist culture. This modern world system, both in its practical
operations and in its ideological self-justifications, simply cannot register the wisdom inherent in any indigenous culture. Modern commercial society is just far too weak a vehicle through which to express
ourselves or to satisfy any of our longings for essential life. Moreover,
the constant transformation of values into commodities actively frus-
trates any sense of a stable and transcendant order to things.

The figures examined here are important because they are living
evidence that it is possible to win back the sublimity of our traditions
without abandoning our hard-won knowledge of their limitations and
excesses. They prove that we can gain a new perspective on our historical predicament that is capable of refurbishing the heroics of the deep
self without capitulating to the premodern vices of superstition, sentimentality, or acquiescence.

In the following chapters I describe this ethic in greater detail as it
is embodied in the lives and work of six plebeian postmodernists. And
although I define this term more fully in Chapter 1, let me just say here
that these figures are plebeian in the sense that they reflect the values
and aspirations of a people, not a party; of a cultural tradition, not an
ideology. And they are postmodern in the sense that although they
accept the modernist critique of classical metaphysics, they go beyond
it by criticizing the expropriation of traditional notions of the sacred
into the reductive categories of modern social science and economics.
Taken together, these figures reveal a tradition of constructive postmodern thought that has its roots in nineteenth-century social
criticism—in Leo Tolstoy, John Ruskin, and Henry David Thoreau—
and comes of age in the twentieth century in the life and work of

Mahatma Gandhi and in other religious reformers who have disclosed a new world within the shell of the already "old" modern one. In Chapter 1, I define this ethic more fully and examine its role in contemporary intellectual history.

In Chapter 2, I examine the ethical pluralism embodied in Gandhi's religious views and the unique power of nonviolence to purge the plebeian vices at the very moment it accentuates plebeian virtues. I argue here that nonviolence is essentially plebeian in that it is based upon the dignity of the person and the reality of the spiritual life. It makes no sense from a materialist perspective; it is inherently metaphysical. On the other hand, nonviolence is not, as some critics have assumed, an essentialism in its own right—prone to all the modernist criticisms of foundational philosophies. On the contrary, it is an anti-foundationalist ethic that transcends the essentialist/existentialist opposition. It is more a form of poetic making than it is a method or tactic.

In Chapter 3, I consider Solzhenitsyn's *Gulag Archipelago* as the antitext to Sartre's *Critique of Dialectical Reason.* Solzhenitsyn criticises dialectics from the vantage point of those who have suffered its most extreme miscalculation—the prisoners of the Stalinist prison camps. His attempt to rewrite the history of the Russian people without generating the same kind of reduction to abstraction born of Marxist totalizations leads him to his "experiment" in literary form. In this experiment metaphor and symbol, coupled with a multitude of actual-life narratives, generate a plebeian aesthetic that offers an authentic alternative to both socialist realism and literary modernism. As in the chapter on Gandhi, the focus here is upon how those who seem excluded from participating in modern history actually see through its pretenses far more clearly than those of us locked within its self-descriptions.

In Chapter 4, I complete my introduction to the intellectual foundations of plebeian postmodernism by examining the idea of the people as it is expressed in the works of Elie Wiesel. His work articulates the dialogue between Jewish traditions of the deep self and the horrors of the Holocaust. Moreover, his defense of the person via Hasidic tale and narrative help to define plebeian postmodernism as a spiritual wager deeply linked to the literary idiom.

The next three chapters focus upon plebeian activists. They demonstrate how practical deeds, as much as arguments and art, generate constructive responses to modernist dilemmas. The chapter on Walesa, for example, shows that constructive action can and should be undertaken on the basis of one's deepest values, whether or not one knows any theory that supports those values. First one stands up for justice— the qualifications, justifications and philosophical implications follow.

In fact, in this case, Walesa's fallibility becomes one of the preconditions for leadership, confirming Henri Nouwen's remark that it is not in self-sufficiency but in creative interdependency that the mystery of life unfolds to us.[4] I go on to draw explicit contrasts between Walesa and Gramsci's idea of the organic intellectual.

In the chapter on Mother Teresa, I examine the difficulty that people have in comprehending plebeian spiritual values, even when they are so beautifully articulated in the life of a near saint. Using Malcolm Muggeridge's essays to reveal this contrast, I explore Muggeridge's attempts to render Mother Teresa's practical Christian ethic accessible to theory-obsessed moderns and then examine the implications that her simple words and deeds hold as a criticism of modern social policies.

In the chapter on Martin Luther King, Jr., I explore specific ways to effect change, meet evil, and transform oneself and one's conditions within a religious plebeian perspective. King's life and work, not to mention the entire civil rights movement in the late fifties and early sixties, is a fountain of examples, metaphors, and parables demonstrating the power of ordinary brave individuals to redeem their times and resuscitate sacred living. As one of the great educators and unsung theologians of our day, King spoke the plebeian sublime with mythic grandeur, courage, and heroic certitude.

In the last two chapters, I examine in greater detail the linkages between these six figures. In Chapter 8, I consider their responses to the disutilities of modernism; in Chapter 9, I focus upon their shared affirmations.

Of course, I could have selected other figures to exemplify plebeian postmodernism—Archbishop Desmond Tutu and Václav Havel come immediately to mind. But one has to stop somewhere, and these six figures seem to me adequate, if not constructively contrasting, examples of the ethic I wish to describe. Each shares the view that there is a fascist within as well as without and that the human shadow is not open to mere intellectual instruction. Political reaction, like personal neurosis, is a shifting, ever-changing unknown that must be confronted again and again if authentic social progress is ever to be achieved.

Moreover, each of these figures recognizes that the values of western civilization have become confused with its existing institutions which have themselves been transformed by the reductive and materialist imperatives of the largely amoral modernist agenda. And so at the very same time each of them affirms the traditional values of community, human dignity, individuality, and historical continuity, she or he also works for change, reform, and revolution.

CHAPTER ONE

Ignorant Perfection

*The Westerner, after centuries of extroverted
science, and determined philosophical attempts to
remove soul from conversation, architecture,
observation and education, sees inside himself, and
sees what the ancients saw, but can hardly believe
it. He confesses that he must be seeing wrong.*

—ROBERT BLY[1]

In an essay written in 1969, Georg Lukács described the works of
Alexander Solzhenitsyn as representative of what Marx called
"plebeianism"—an ethic that expressed "the ignorant perfection of
ordinary people."[2] Ordinary people—those not privileged by extraordinary wealth, power, or position—were perfect in that they saw
through the frauds and tyrannies of their day. But they were also
ignorant in that they didn't know where those tyrannies came from or
what to do about them. For Marx and Lukács, plebeians simply did not
possess the sense of history or the dispassionate scientific method to
understand their place in the sociopolitical scheme of things.[3] Mystified by the market (or misled by propaganda), ordinary people suc-
cumbed to simplistic explanations that distorted their understanding of
experience and perverted their moral instincts. This lack of critical
consciousness made them easy prey to ideologies that fed their parochial self-interests and tendencies toward self-aggrandizement. Religion was to be their predictable opiate, and fascism their grand
temptation.

Marx wanted to educate the masses beyond this ignorance—and
inoculate them against fascism—by subjecting to criticism the ideologies that constituted their mystification. Dialectical materialism was
to give intellectual authority to what the people instinctively already
knew: that *real* life, the life of concrete human relationships, empirical,
moral, common life is the base upon which all else stands. And if this
life, as it was experienced *by the people*, was unjust or ignoble, then no
explanatory ideology, theory, or religion should be allowed to stand in

the way of honest reform. In fact, if any theory did explain away injustice that, in itself, was proof that it was an expression of "false consciousness."

But the irony here is that Marx ended up discrediting popular experience at the very moment he sought to redeem it. By adopting materialist premises and turning Hegel right-side up, Marx modernized the dogmas of nineteenth-century natural science, making them new, setting them into historical motion, and inscribing ontology within their reductionist epistemological parameters. Dialectics rather than consensus or conscience became the key to reality. This move eliminated personal intuition, common sense, memory, moral outrage, and ordinary language as valid sources of truth. From a dialectical perspective, such expressions were fatally compromised by the accidents of history and the illogic of the masses. Lacking any scientific foundation, popular consciousness and the will of the people could be more or less dismissed as inevitably reactionary. Marx put it this way:

> The tradition of all the dead generations weighs like a nightmare on the brain of the living. And just when they seem engaged in revolutionizing themselves and things, in creating something that never existed, precisely in such periods of revolutionary crisis they anxiously conjure up the spirits of the past to their service and borrow from them names, battle cries and costumes in order to present the new scene of world history in this time-honoured disguise and this borrowed language.[4]

Thus even in the most revolutionary of times people tend to fall back on what they know, and what they know, sadly enough, is the history and language of mystification. From this perspective, the entire Romantic movement in the nineteenth-century, like all popular revolutions of consciousness, was never anything more than conservative nostalgia, doomed from the start to be an ineffectual protest against the brave new industrial world. So unless ordinary people were initiated into the method of dialectical analysis, by definition they were incapable of knowing what was happening to them in any ethical or abstract sense. From the world-historical perspective of the whole, what seemed like injustice and deprivation might actually be just. And what seemed like lies, distortions, and deceptions might just be the necessary dialectical corrections needed to carry forward the unfolding wisdom of the evolving historical totality.

The disorienting effects of such moral inversions were brilliantly dramatized in Arthur Koestler's *Darkness At Noon* and in the works of

George Orwell, Alexander Solzhenitsyn, Milan Kundera, and that whole panoply of Eastern European artists and intellectuals (one might even include Georg Lukács here) whose personal sense of truth and integrity clashed with Marxist philosophic hubris.[5] Their works made it abundantly clear that at the very moment Marx corrected plebeian ignorance, he destroyed any sense of plebeian perfection.

This disillusionment might not have been so bad had it issued merely in a new skepticism toward the pieties of bourgeois society. But coupled to the positivist and utilitarian orientation of the Victorian mind, Marx's critique gave birth to a totalizing, and eventually totalitarian, philosophy harboring all the ancient vices of the Gnostic heresy. Marxist *cognoscenti* reinterpreted all problems as ritualized ideological conflicts to be overcome through political interventions.

This inversion of Marxism from liberating critique to oppressive state philosophy, coming as it did not so long after capitalism had already erased the spirituality of the Christian Middle Ages, generated an ethical vacuum in the common, practical life of Western civilization. There could be no simple return to the values of the past, and yet no revolution in good conscience. We had entered an age of relativism and fanaticism where the best lacked all conviction, the worst were full of passionate intensity, and ordinary people—to paraphrase Santayana—oscillated between a radical transcendentalizing (reduced to a solipsism of the living moment) and a materialism posited as a presupposition of conventional sanity.[6] Unlike the philosopher, most ordinary people bounced back and forth between these poles unknowingly with classic bourgeois duplicity, still believing themselves to be integrated persons of faith or persons of reason, when in fact, they were more truly mirrors of the prevailing cultural schizophrenia: torn between the mobile freedom of modernization and the anxiety for order characteristic of the displaced Victorian mind.

As Philip Rieff so deftly described in *The Triumph of the Therapeutic* (1966) ordinary moderns negotiated an uneasy, often disingenuous, truce between the world they revered and the world they lived in and had become, denying the vast abyss between their actions and their ideals. Any pretense of plebeian perfection had long since been rejected as the sentimental excesses of an obsolete humanism. Private therapies replaced common culture as the means for self-perfection and ethical accomplishment.

Some avant-garde critics of ordinary life such as Theodore Adorno and Jurgen Habermas were so taken by the extent of modern false consciousness and bad faith that they came to the conclusion that not only were ordinary people inauthentic, but persons as such really didn't even exist and perhaps they never had existed. What really exists are structures, residual existential projects, the debris of past institutional needs, sign systems, and ideologies, all of which presses upon the brain of the body politic like a nightmare. In a modernist rendition of the old Marxist project, they sought to refurbish dialectics from the inside out, using more sophisticated analytical tools borrowed from such fields as linguistics, cybernetics, psychoanalysis, and even artificial intelligence.[7]

Orthodox Marxism, therefore, did not really resolve the tension between the plebeian longing for universal justice and the conditional circumstances of social life. It merely defined this paradox away, deferred it to another time, and so drove moral rebellion underground. In our day this tension has reemerged in a whole series of popular uprisings, from Tiananmen Square to the Gdansk shipyards. Dialectical materialism itself has been exposed as a tool for the mystification of the masses as alienating as any other form of false consciousness. However refined its analyses of the anthropological origins of values or however complex its descriptions of multilayered mediations, dialectics still sees common, everyday human experience as an epiphenomenon of more fundamental realities that are accessible only to its own special methodology. Thus, Marxism continues to exclude from serious consideration commonsense appeals by ordinary people to alter its programs, adapt its agenda, or acknowledge a reality outside its materialist ken.

And yet cultural theorists and activists did emerge who sought to preserve the perfection of ordinary people by bringing the traditions of, let us call it, "the deep self" into dialogue with contemporary history. I am speaking of religious plebeian activists such as Gandhi and Martin Luther King and politically progressive personalists such as Emmanuel Mounier and Martin Buber, who accepted the modern criticisms of plebeian ethnocentricism, sentimentality, and self-interest but rejected the materialist and reductionist premises of such critiques in favor of a more constructive philosophy. Like Stephen Dedalus, they sought to fly by the nets of parochial family life, jingoistic nationalism, and superstitious religious practice. But unlike Joyce's hero, they did not fly into the silence, exile, and cunning of the modernist mind, but into the redeemed narrative speech and mythic return of the plebeian postmodern. Let me explain.

Modernists, like Joyce, saw themselves as residing at a turning point in history, if not at its climax. Their theories miniaturized the past and took it up as an element of the present, dissolving its structures, revealing its hidden dynamics, and announcing a new age. Whether that new age was characterized by the Kantian revolution, the Hegelian completion of philosophy, or the Surrealist manifesto, it amounted to the same thing: a tearing down of the old cultural foundations in order to replace them with something new, something more inclusive and less self-deceived.

Modernism had its hopeful side in a positivist faith in progress and its pessimistic side in a rebellious concern with the existential meaning of our cultural disinheritance. Both sides, however, shared the same sense of historical discontinuity and the same preoccupation with the foundations of knowledge and culture. Through their aesthetic and philosophic experiments they succeeded in exposing the epistemological hubris of existing religious traditions, their classical allies, and any new emergent essentialisms.

Unfortunately, their successes had the effect of turning western civilization away from any common collective moral life—the life Marx's plebeians revered—toward a multiplicity of disciplines, specializations, jargons, and, in the realm of aesthetics, bohemian sects. The art world found itself awash in a plurality of virtuoso performances and over-determined creations that contained within their structures their own theoretical self-justifications. The works of Igor Stravinsky and Pablo Picasso, for example, contained within them their own immanent teleologies. While political leaders found themselves rummaging through the fragments of a thousand renounced ideologies, searching for some fact or premise to shore up discredited institutions or to justify bloody revolutions. The old mythologies were to be replaced by new methodologies, and these methodologies were to be grounded in theoretically self-conscious sciences, either experimental or phenomenological. Ordinary life ceased to be ordinary, and schizophrenia became the ontological rule rather than the psychological exception.

Nonetheless, many plebeian thinkers out of loyalty to their heritage resist such a usurpation of posterity. They read the present as a moment of historical recurrence miniaturized, in you will, in the ancient memory-aesthetic of the tribe: an aesthetic embodied in the re-collective idioms of myth, narrative, ritual, and symbol. These idioms do not so much assume the significance of direct experience as create it. Moreover they exist in a time beyond mere chronological time, in a time that is not so much eternal as omni-temporal.[8]

What distinguished these new plebeian apologists from their predecessors was that they sought to reaffirm historical continuity, the reality of the person, and the value of common experience by moving more deeply into the modernist recognition that all of us are the products of particular national, historical, psychological, and religious contexts and consequently our existence is as much defined by our roots, our ethnicity, and our difference as it is by our existential freedom to remake ourselves. They asserted, moreover, that as different as our roots and peculiarities might be, all of us share certain hard-core, commonsensical premises that define a resistant and resilient humanism. These premises include the notion that persons should never be treated merely as means but always as ends and the idea that since life ends in death, its meaning and significance must transcend mere material well-being.

And so these postmodern plebeians offer a qualified yes-and-no to the modernist outlook: yes to its critique of classical absolutes, but no to its radical usurpation of posterity into the reductive categories of materialist science, and no to its dissolution of direct experience into the problematics of epistemology. They reject the apocalyptic historicism in modernism without rejecting history itself. Their way of thinking resembles the thought before history, which is myth, and the thought outside of history, which is mysticism; and yet it is neither, because its main concern is with concrete events in all their manifest particularity.

In other words, plebeian postmoderns psychologize and spiritualize the ancient traditions by particularizing and qualifying their claims; at the same time they subject modernity itself to a historical accounting. Their perspective is an amalgam of traditionalist virtues linked to an agenda of social reform and brought up to date through a dialectical yes and no to the modernist critique of metaphysics. This perspective rejects elitism and romantic excess for pragmatic, prudent loyalties. It is a view of the world from the ground up, an urge to universality within the constraints of the particular. It is the Beatitudes. The poet before the philosopher. Solzhenitsyn over Lukács. Walesa before Gorbachev. It is the awareness that our humanity is neither a fiction nor a birthright but an ethical accomplishment.

The great plebeian theme is not alienation, but the problematics of assimilation—surviving modernity without giving up too much of that rich blend of commitments and obligations that constitute one's heritage, one's spirituality, one's character, one's best self. Put most simply, *plebeian postmodernism* represents the awakened consciousness of common men and women to their need to find their own bearings in history without sacrificing their sense of the sacred.

The revelation here is that our true being resides neither within us encoded in some special psychological destiny, nor high above above us in abstract revolutionary ideals, but rather all around us, perpetually at hand in our families, our pasts, our public and private lives, our rites and our works, and in our possibilities and responsibilities. For it is in these concrete, particular matters that the world addresses us, asks us who we are, and calls upon us to recollect our origins with gratitude and a resolute love of life.

Gandhi found himself addressed by the Indian masses; Martin Luther King Jr. by the African-American Church; Solzhenitsyn, by the zeks of the Soviet gulag; Mother Teresa, by the poorest of the poor on the streets of Calcutta, and Elie Wiesel, by the Jews of Auschwitz and Buchenwald. The concrete values, commitments, and existential absolutes that emerged from these encounters offer us a way of resisting the reductive materialism of the prevailing powers without betraying those who have gone before or those who are yet to come. Moreover, the particular perspectives that emerge from such historically situated ethical projects make us sensitive to the sufferings of others, and increase, rather than limit, our sense of solidarity with all peoples.

Plebeian postmodernism is, thus, reflected in a consortium of thinkers and doers who share an ethic that honors the concrete deed before the abstract stance and the claims of the family before the fictions of the state. It judges the quality of one's practice by the good it concretely accomplishes rather than by the party it serves, the money it makes, or the coherence of the theory upon which it is based. And it refuses the claim that concrete good cannot be defined, for good is defined every day in feeding the hungry and ministering to the sick. Plebeian postmodernism is an ethic existing within time, unfolding in history, rather than an atemporal system floating in abstract philosophical space. This is one reason why it is so much easier to illustrate than to define.

Plebeian postmodernism does not just represent a populist political orientation or the survival of the religious sensibility in its perennial clash with the untransformed world. The ethic stands for an inclusive complex of preindustrial values, mytho-poetic practices, and humanist categories of thought that have survived into our time as sanctuaries of the sacred, making up what Lech Walesa once referred to as effective immunities against the totalitarian plague.[9] The totalitarian plague refers not just to totalitarian governments and institutions but also to the mind-set that wishes to escape "the judgement of the past and our responsibility for past injustice."[10] Totalitarianism is, in this sense, more a psychological orientation, a species of folly, than it is a political philosophy.

Plebeian values and categories, in so far as they are expressions of traditional cultural practices qualified by common sense and practical need, resist this folly and cut across international boundaries to link indigenous peoples to First-World plebeians and progressive postmoderns. The right-left political spectrum which had emerged from the assumption that modernization was the fundamental political reality has now been superceeded by a new politics that redefines the political axis in terms of the contradictions between folk cultures and empire, between the plebeian desire for a meaningful life and the desire of market managers to erase as many moral and space-time distinctions as possible from the commercial environment.[11] The question is no longer, How fast we should modernize or even whether we dare to modernize; rather the question is, What we can salvage of human dignity and meaning in a modernized world? How can our souls survive our histories?

The movement postmodern plebeianism represents is not from liberal humanism to religious mysticism; rather it seeks to reconcile the egalitarian forces of history with the the aristocratic ideals built into traditional notions of the self. Postmodern plebeians seek reform, but not at the expense of the heroic standard that judges virtue by accomplishment. They stand counter to any parties and philosophical schemes that would explain away their moral and spiritual aspirations as belonging to another time or lesser reality. They affirm the self at the same time as they affirm equality by stressing the sanctity of the individual. They refuse to collapse character into culture or morality into private life. For them the fullest individuality issues in the most developed social conscience. To paraphrase Martin Luther King Jr., plebeian postmoderns agree that one has not started to live until one has ceased to identify with one's private problems so as to identify with the sufferings of all humanity.

The destruction of the old metaphysic that so worried our noble Victorian forebears and gave birth to such mighty works of moral reflection as Thomas Carlyle's *Sartor Resartus* (1830), John Cardinal Newman's *Apologia Pro Vita* (1864), and Matthew Arnold's *Culture and Anarchy* (1868), has led to neither nihilism nor Leninism nor positivism but, in the case of the figures examined here, to a brave resistance to all three in the name of human solidarity and nonviolence. Whole nations within nations have refused to give up their gods, but not failed to redefine their roles in history. As a result a new kind of historical consciousness is emerging, which is represented by ordinary people living out extraordinary ideals. These people hold to ancient ethical values without superstition and seek to perfect a practical form of spirituality that does not evade the challenges of the modern world but rather meets them on its own soul-centered terms with remorseless self-honesty.

CHAPTER TWO

Gandhi: Nonviolence as Poetic Making

> *Love in action is a harsh and dreadful thing*
> *compared to love in dreams. Love in dreams is*
> *greedy for immediate action, rapidly performed and*
> *in the sight of all. Men will give their lives if only*
> *the ordeal does not last long but is soon over, with*
> *all looking and applauding as though on stage. But*
> *active love is labour and fortitude, and for some*
> *people, too, perhaps a complete science. But I*
> *predict that just when you see with horror that in*
> *spite of all your efforts you are getting further from*
> *your goal instead of nearer to it—at that very*
> *moment you will reach and behold clearly the*
> *miraculous power of the Lord who has been all the*
> *time loving and mysteriously guiding you.*
>
> —FATHER ZOSSIMA IN
> DOSTOEVSKY'S *Brothers Karamazov*[1]

The great plebeian values are God, family, memory, conscience, and character. The great plebeian vices are authoritarianism, ethnocentricism, superstition, provincialism, and self-righteousness. Postmodern plebeian leaders have sought ways to preserve the plebeian virtues while minimizing their vices. First among these techniques is Gandhian nonviolence, for it offers ordinary people a way of fighting for change without adopting the very depersonalizing tactics they are struggling against and so without betraying the ideals of their own sacred traditions by becoming like those they oppose.

The genius of nonviolence resides in its profound psychological understanding of how our refusal to feel what we really feel and our ambitions to be other than who we are doom us to an inner anxiety that feeds both political and psychological oppression. But if we can learn to side with truth—not only against our enemies but also against ourselves and our own fears and ambitions, we can learn to suffer creatively—that is to say, productively. And by so doing, we can remain true to the ethical lessons taught us by our own communities of origin and thus achieve liberation in the moment by entering into a dialogue with God's inscrutable will in history.

Nonviolence keys on two primary plebeian strengths: the will to a life of virtue and the acceptance of one's inevitable human fallibility. Unlike violence, nonviolence cannot be put into the service of sweeping ideological denunciations because it undermines self-righteousness by insisting that one perpetually refine one's moral distinctions as they evolve dialectically in confrontation with others. And unlike dialectics, nonviolence centers upon the heroic individual conscience as the guiding light of creative social progress and so eschews authoritarian movements as insufficiently sensitive to the unfolding experiential wisdom of the existentially engaged soldier of truth.

By its emphasis upon remaining true to one's own indigenous experience and suffering out the consequences of one's own sense of virtue, nonviolence directly assaults sentimental religious pieties and superstitions that exploit the desire for extraordinary states of consciousness. Like meditation, it teaches one to sit quietly in the center of the world storm—immoveable, patient, and resolute. To the status quo, nonviolence may appear disruptive, unsettling, even revolutionary, but its goals are a postmodern blending of cultures, a pastiche, an accommodation of competing traditions that does not compromise moral essences.

In his essay "Gandhi, Politics, and Us," Martin Buber describes the unique contribution nonviolence makes to the resolution of the conflict between the infinite spiritual aspirations of human beings and their limited institutional environments. He points out that just before the riots of Chauri Chaura broke out in February of 1922, the British were on the verge of capitulating to Gandhi's ultimatum for self rule. Their prisons were full, and they had little influence over the three-hundred and nineteen million Indian nationals. But after the riots took place—even though he was on the verge of victory—Gandhi withdrew his ultimatum to the Viceroy, describing the violence as a warning from God "that there does not yet exist in India the truthful and nonviolent atmosphere that alone can justify mass disobedience."[2]

Buber points out that in refusing to exploit human passions for immediate victory, Gandhi acknowledged a higher value than mere political success. For Gandhi, social change without inner transformation is not change at all, but merely a furthering of the growing duality of politics and religion symptomatic of the modern rift between ethics and action. Political change must be accompanied by a change in values based upon actual insight into one's codependent condition, or it would only further separate the Indian masses from their best selves and enshrine a government as blind to moral realities as the one that it replaced.

Unlike Marx, who absorbed religion into politics, and unlike the Moral Majority, whose professed goal was to "politicize" conservative Christians, Gandhi wanted to temper politics itself by absorbing it into the universal wisdom of the Gita—in other words, to undermine the ubiquitous power of politics through adherence to the deeper more inclusive religious truths of tolerance and humility before God. "I seem to take part in politics," Gandhi said. "But this is only because politics today strangles us like the coils of a serpent out of which one cannot slip whatever one tries. I desire, therefore, to wrestle with a serpent."[3]

Of all the political creeds of the twentieth century, only non-violence addresses the contradiction between "the unconditionality of the spirit and the conditionality of a situation."[4] It does not resolve this tension—only God could do that—but it keeps political participants aware that it exists and thereby works to minimize the danger that they will confuse their immediate ends with God's destination or ignore the will of God altogether to engage in cynical power plays.

Martin Luther King found this notion of a struggle tragically poised between the conditionality of history and the unconditionality of God's will so vital that he had all of the volunteers in the Birmingham movement sign a commitment card that contained ten commandments for nonviolent action. Commandment number two read: "REMEMBER always that the nonviolent movement in Birmingham seeks justice and reconciliation—not victory."[5] To seek victory would only politicize the people at the cost of mobilizing their vices. But if you set justice and reconciliation as your goal, you link the struggle of your people to the broader concerns of all humanity and thereby directly assault the plebeian vices of provincialism and parochial self-interest. Nonviolence is, in this sense, a spiritual discipline, not just a tactic. In it plebeian existential rebellion finds an ethic within which it can discover its own excesses and limitations and thereby move with self-correcting surety against the tyrannies of its world.

What the secular world wants, from Gandhi's perspective, is not at all what the soul needs. And so a tension is set up between the greatness of humanity's spiritual aspirations and the mean-spirited environment we call "history." This paradox is the source of the ignorant perfection of ordinary people described by Marx. But for Gandhi, this paradox constitutes the crucifiction of ordinary persons' inner lives—not their political backwardness. And, for Gandhi, its resolution resides in a spiritual awakening, in ahimsa—in overcoming this duality through conscious suffering and nonviolent noncooperation with evil.

octic

It was on this very point that George Orwell criticized Gandhi's politics:

> Gandhi's teachings cannot be squared with the belief that man is the measure of all things and that our job is to make life worth living on earth, which is the only earth we have. They make sense only on the assumption that God exists and that the world of solid objects is an illusion to be escaped from. . . . One must choose between God and Man, and all radicals and progressives from the mildest liberal to the most extreme Anarchist, have in effect chosen man.[6]

Orwell may be right when he says that Gandhi's ideas cannot be squared with the belief that "man" is the measure of all things, but he is wrong to say that his ideas cannot be squared with our job to make life on earth worth living. If anything, religion for Gandhi was the unflagging quest to perfect one's soul in service to God as manifested in life on earth. The two cannot be separated. In fact, it is one of the functions of the poetry of scripture and the ascetic practices of prayer and fasting to help us to unlearn the established antinomies between the practical and the theoretical and the sacred and the profane.

We do not yet know what humanity is nor who God is, so how can we choose between them? We can only grope toward human approximations by living out our own experiments in truth. Gandhi does not define an ethic or even affirm some other worldly ideology so much as live on the edge of his own evolving inquiry into the nature and value of classical Hindu precepts. His is an existential search for the limits of virtue in himself and in humanity. "What is possible for me," he claims, "is possible for everybody." The catch here is that what is possible for Gandhi is as yet unknown—yet to be established in practice and, so, open-ended. The recipe of noncooperation with evil is not a recipe for moral perfection so much as a prescription for personal authenticity. It is a way, not to gain power, but to remain faithful to oneself.

As to Orwell's claims that the world of solid objects is an illusion for Gandhi, one might better say that, for Gandhi, the world of industrially produced commercial objects is an illusion. British hegemony, like the desacralization of the plebeian traditions, comes as much in the form of manufactured goods, schools, and hospitals as it does from soldiers and bureaucrats. And although they laughed at Gandhi's cloth spinning movement, it was symbolic of his insight that the entire service-delivery system of Western civilization was disabling to India's great masses because it created new needs and new poverties and fostered the illusion that people can attain happiness by purchasing goods and services. Such a worldview is based upon economic models that ignore use-values. In other words, the more advanced the masses become in Western economic terms, the more enslaved they are to alienating modern needs. But needs for such "solid objects" *are* illusory, argues Gandhi, if they are bought at the price of one's liberty and self-determination.

Orwell's reading of Gandhi looks at his ideas through a modern Western framework, focusing upon their implicit eschatology, absolutism, and mystic antirationalism. But Gandhi did not see his own thought in those terms. His asceticism was a way of failing to absorb the Western industrial ethic gracefully. If history was to break him in the end, why not let it break him in the service of his most profound understanding of human virtue, not in an appropriation of the most reductive categories of human understanding imaginable in a futile quest to mollify Western politicians.

Orwell may well object that virtue in the absolute must sometimes be sacrificed for the sake of specific friends and individual loyalties, and that any program that tries to surpass this limiting condition is itself totalitarian. Gandhi's asceticism does, in this sense, broach the totalitarian temptation. But Gandhi's saving grace is that the practice of nonviolence, like prayer or meditation, is not a static repetition of a value but part of a dialectic. As a conversation with God's will in history it is open-ended—it is not a method in a Western sense. It is a way of continuing dialogue and relationship after words cease to matter. It enlarges one's understanding of the meaning of one's actions at the very moment one is acting. It is not an assertion of limits; it is a limit testing act. It is a kind of practice, an art. It requires dedication, self-knowledge, honesty, and insight; it cannot be repeated in the laboratory because it is intimately engaged with the immediate and hence unique historical moment.

In Gandhi's nonviolent campaigns the enemy was seen as a mirror of aspects of oneself that one needed to confront and absorb rather than merely reject. The enemy is, in a strange way, one's collaborator against social evil. The nonviolent warrior goes into battle against injustice *with* his Jungian shadow, not against it. The goal is not to eliminate others but to transform them into friends. And this is no mere trick to lead them to compromise their principles; for Gandhi, one must be willing to change oneself, to give in to reason, to respond to the kindnesses of others, to compromise and seek mutuality, and to suffer out the consequences of living for truths someone else denies or cannot see.

Gandhian postmodern plebeians are, in this sense, both essentialists and existentialists. Since they believe God's transcendental unity is beyond all knowing, they trust in the plurality of cultural expressions as limited heuristics upon which to base existential errands for God. They are critical situationalists working within their own immediate contexts; no greater totalization is just, no other authenticity is possible. And so nonviolence becomes the common sense limit to their own assertion of political will.

Perhaps the most moving scene in Richard Attenborough's film *Gandhi* occurs during Gandhi's fast in protest of Moslem–Hindu violence in January 1948. In the film a Hindu comes to Gandhi in tears, telling him that he would gladly die in Gandhi's place for his life has become worthless. Gandhi, upon inquiry, discovers that the man's little boy was killed by Moslems, and in rage and despair this man attacked the first Moslem child he saw, bashing its head against a wall.

Gandhi replies that he thinks he knows a way out of hell for this suffering man. The man must find a child orphaned by the rioting and raise that child as his own. But what is more—he must adopt a Moslem child and raise the orphan *as a Moslem*.[7] The shock of recognition in the suffering man's eyes is one of the great moments in this film, for in an instant the poetic justice of Gandhi's insight strikes home, and the man knows what he must do.

This little scene is more than just good cinema, for embedded in it is the essence of Gandhi's postmodern ethic. A premodern Christian priest would have found it hard to recommend raising a child as a Moslem under any circumstances. A modern psychoanalyst could have only offered the man therapy, dialogue, long-term reeducation. A Marxist might have framed the event historically—explaining its social origins and, perhaps, ameliorating some of the guilt by transferring it onto circumstance. An existentialist might have appealed to the man's freedom to choose a new, more responsible life in recompense. But each of these appeals falls short, for each begs this man's fundamental question: Having killed, what right have I to live? Having fallen so low, how dare I aspire again to a moral life?

The answer Gandhi gave in the film is of an entirely different order than any of the ones previously mentioned, for it is at once prescriptive yet relative, absolute yet conditional, existential yet essentialist, dogmatic yet relativistic—honoring religious faiths as transparent mythologies at the very moment it deconstructs them as fundamentalist dogmas—healing a man at the very moment he challenges him.

Here is a new synthesis of the ancient and the modern in a pragmatic plebeian ethic keyed to the spiritual aspirations of the ordinary brave soul. It exemplifies the plebeian partisanship toward the mythic and its firm belief that all religious traditions affirm essentially the same truths.

Gandhi remarked,

> Supposing a Christian came to me and said he was captivated by reading of Bhagavat and so wanted to declare himself a Hindu, I should say to him: "No. What Bhagavat offers, the Bible also offers. You have not made the attempt to find it out. Make the attempt and be a good Christian."[8]

That is to say, make the attempt to go beyond the doctrines and surfaces of you own tradition-bound scriptures to their spiritual essence—an essence you can perhaps see more clearly in the scriptures of other traditions like the Gita because there are less preemptive institutional interpretations to deal with, less secondary misreadings, less doctrinal overlay, less history, and less politics. But note that Gandhi still advises us to return to *our own* scriptures because the story of their despiritualization is the story of our own alienation and religious cooptation. The contested context of these texts is an important part of their meaning for us.

Thus for Gandhi, Westerners should recognize how the most visionary texts in their tradition have been used to defend such inhuman practices as slavery. It is important to take back the gospel from that nineteenth century "Christian" slave owner who upon returning from his summer religious retreat used to beat Fredrick Douglass, and from those contemporary religious leaders who have taught us to equate God's love for us with doctrines of cultural superiority, exclusivity, and special privilege.[9]

There is a lesson for our time here as we struggle to reconcile our traditions with the radical modern critiques of their historical and philosophical foundations. The hermeneutic strategy of plebeian spiritual religion as practiced by Gandhi offers us a way to reaffirm as we deconstruct. For Gandhi truth means advaita, nonduality, the spiritual unity realized through nonviolence and the practice of love—not the indisputable fact or the undoubtable premise. Competing traditions are assessed in relationship to a dehistoricized truth—not in relationship to each other.

Admittedly, this is a controversial strategy. In a modern analytic criticism of Gandhi's doctrines William Borman points out several irreconcilable contradictions within Gandhi's thought.[10] Gandhi's rigid adherence to the belief that nonviolence is always preferable to violence, for example, is shown to rest upon a circular argument. Gandhi, he claims, asserts the equivalence of the microcosm with the macrocosm and by extension the ideal with the real without ever really arguing for either claim. Then Gandhi goes on to build from these premises the argument that all violence fails practically because it does not advance moral aims, and that nonviolence, although it sometimes leads to loss of life, never fails in practice—because it always affirms the ideal.

But, Borman points out, such a claim does not really refute the idea that two wrongs can make a right. Also, it does not provide us with any practical guidelines for judging when a violent act may be more moral than a nonviolent one that in itself leads to loss of life. Since loss of life is not the ultimate value and automatic guiding principle for him, Gandhi's practical ethics clash with his moral metaphysics, reopening the question of balancing good with evil. "Gandhi merely constructs his moral-metaphysical 'laws' to objectify his *a priori* valuations and validate his methods, practical philosophy and claims."[11] In short, Gandhi is an ideologue and mythmaker and, moreover, a dangerous one in that the more inspirational he is, the more difficult it becomes to draw important moral distinctions about the use and abuse of violence. Although Borman gives Gandhi the man great credit for his courage and political achievements, as a philosopher Gandhi fails because he replaces commonsense assessments with ideological axioms that simply lack convincing support.

But for Gandhi ahimsa was never a method—it was more a wager, a poetic. And although he called upon the name of science to invest his "experiments" in nonviolence with intellectual prestige, he was more truly composing a great drama on the stage of world history. His experiments were actually ideological inquiries, bits of propaganda in the making, self-confirming artifacts.

To the postmodern sensibility this is not as damning an admission as it might first appear. Gandhi's confusion of realms was, in fact, a creative construct and an affirmation designed to help modern humanity unlearn the antinomies that had hitherto controlled their lives. His conflation of the ideal and the real, however magical and intellectually unjustifiable, neither resolved nor transcended these oppositions but, like a good modernist poem, made them reciprocally evocative. In other words, Gandhi's experiments in truth were not scientific but aesthetic (in the fullest ethical and philosophical senses of that term). Like the surrealists before him he played with a set of assumptions to see what they might produce—only, his canvas was the world, and his medium, politics.

He was essentially a maker in the Aristotelian sense, not a theorist. He must be granted his givens and judged by his fruits. The fact that part of his fruits was a body of theory justifies Borman's criticisms from a strictly analytical view. But most of Gandhi's creations were moral and political deeds, and they must stand or fall on the historical record as unique actual occasions. It may be that his deeds ultimately failed to change history because they were based on logically confused assumptions; on the other hand, they may have already changed the lives we lead, not only by bringing about India's independence from England peacefully, but also by erasing certain philosophical oppositions previously built into our traditional self-descriptions. But this is a very different problem than whether or not his arguments are logically consistent.

The "laws" of satyagraha were never scientific laws so much as transcendental deductions in the Kantian sense. They are justified by their capacity to make possible "a domain of objectivity." Paul Ricoeur remarks on this process in his work *The Symbolism of Evil*:

> How shall we get beyond the 'circle of hermeneutics'? By transforming it into a *wager*.
> I wager that I shall have a better understanding of man and of all beings if I follow the *indication* of symbolic thought. That wager then becomes the task of verifying my wager and saturating it, so to speak, with intelligibility. In return, the task transforms my wager: in betting on the significance of the symbolic world, I bet at the same time that my wager will be restored to me in power of reflection, in the element of coherent discourse. [12]

Seen in the light of Ricoeur's phenomenology of the will, Gandhi is no mere metaphysical ventriloquist making the world of political experience "say" what he already knows must be true given his religious assumptions. On the contrary, his religious assumptions make it possible to interrogate the world in the light of mankind's traditional, if unfounded, ontological predispositions.

This is a fundamentally different role for thought from the modernist project of constructing a universal history of human development free from anthropomorphism. For Ricoeur, it is the act of responding to the symbols that give rise to thought and "give us reason to think that the *Cogito* is within being, and not vice versa." Gandhi broke "out of the enchanted enclosure of consciousness of oneself, to end the prerogative of self-reflection," and by so doing overcame history as the inescapable precategory of all human meaning. [13]

For Gandhi "history is a record of an interruption of the course of nature. Soul force, being natural, is not noted in history." [14] History is really a record of every interruption of the even working of the force of love or of the soul. The fact that this truth resides outside of history leads Gandhi to advocate a pluralistic perspectivism rather than a strict ethical relativism or absolute skepticism. Any and all expressions of the historical sensibility (that is to say, any expressions of the nonliterary, asymbolic imagination) are inevitably partial, partisan, and *wrong*— caught up as they are in duality and the clash of antagonistic mythologies.

Gandhi's religious assumptions, his "eternal" perspective, his rejection of history, put him in direct opposition not only to captial and empire but to Marxism. In fact, his views on history seem more in agreement with certain developments in postmodern literature than with any recognizable political ideas. Milan Kundera, speaking of contemporary trends in the novel, has said:

> For Cervantes, history was the barely visible background of adventure.
>
> For Balzac, it became a "natural" dimension without which man is unthinkable.
>
> Today, at last, history appears like a monster, ready to assault each of us and destroy the world. Or else (another aspect of its monstrousness), it represents the immeasurable, incomprehensible *mass* of the past—a past which is unbearable as forgetfulness (because man will lose himself), but also as memory (because its mass will crush us).[15]

For Gandhi's soldier of truth, history is the stuff of self-transformation, the material of ethical accomplishment, the baggage standing between ourselves and the eternal. Gandhi did not see history as a nightmare from which we are trying to awake so much as an intrusion in our natural lives. To overcome history we cannot accept its terms, we have to continually assault them. Admittedly this is not easy, nor is it programmatic—that is why Gandhi does not have "answers" for every world-historic dilemma. But he does articulate hitherto unthinkable alternatives.

This sweeping inversion of nature and history coupled as it is with his tactical use of the transcendental deduction makes any positive criticism of Gandhi difficult because one cannot simply show that his ideas are contradictory given competing philosophical assumptions; one has to approach his work as one would the work of an artist— examining the conditions that gave rise to his thought and expression, and explaining why he embraced such seeming contradictions so willingly, so bravely, and so heroically. Moreover, one has to consider how his creative "constructs" situate us with respect to our own lives and being.

Martin Green is one critic who has attempted to do just that, seeking to define a Gandhian aesthetic in a series of books on the lust for power. He sees Gandhi's ahimsa as the spiritual compliment to F. R. Leavis's notion of the Great Tradition. The Great Tradition is the canon of serious works built upon the values lived by "organic communities" and rigorously distinguished from the rest of humanity's expressive acts by philosophically serious critics. Leavis sets the agenda for modern criticism as a resistance to the values of an imperialist world system. But he lacks any real program for change except pointing to the fragments of a lost unity. Gandhi's ahimsa is a proscriptive program for healing such destruction, and his life an heroic example of what can be accomplished in this world at this time with the simple tools of the ancients—nobility, integrity, and soul.

Green defines his own position as a critic navigating by both lights: "The maelstrom of ideas and art (in the modern world) is not merely to be resisted or deplored. It is indeed one of the most wonderful achievements of human culture ever seen. My job is to navigate the maelstrom, to yield to it enough to know it, and discriminate between better and worse."[16] He goes on to say that such politically engaged critical practice "would not be to save the world. The world, it seems, would not be saved by Gandhi, so we need not torment ourselves with such ideas. All we can aim at is to save our honor."[17] In Green's latest work, *The Origins of Nonviolence*,[18] he carries out his own world-historical critique of the West's victory over the conscience of the world.

The satyagrahi recognizes the power of the mind has to leap over all obstacles to an instant, if unreal, realization of its aims in the imagination. It can instantly refute ideas and civilizations that took centuries to develop, and it can just as easily invent aims and values that will take centuries to realize. The thinker must then choose whether to live the unfettered but fantastic life of the mind or the more limited way of the soldier of truth. Most modern critics choose the mind, and so their relationships to their own compromised lives—"compromised" since no life can achieve the utopian aspirations of pure thought—is a heady mixture of contempt, pride, and self-doubt. While those who choose the practical life often either give up abstract thinking altogether or find some creed to protect them from the radical instability of the mind alive.

Gandhi's experiments in truth offer a third way—a life of practical struggle informed by spiritual aspirations that see everyday experiences as challenges to the will and imagination. Domestic problems cease to be distractions from the great work and become object lessons in the power of ahimsa. Simple creeds and religious formulas renew themselves when applied directly to new political controversies. The creative imagination ceases to be an escape from practical life and social obligations because it no longer identifies itself with the absolute freedom of indivdual thought but rather becomes the means through which one achieves inner and outter transformation.

Perhaps Gandhi's Hindu religiosity led him to a too-optimistic faith of the political effects of such consciousness raising, but his plebeian commitment to the particular, human-sized event saved him from any theoretical hubris. For Gandhi, everything was an experiment in truth, a try, an essay. And when he brought the shadow side of the British Empire up to view, he was not suprised to find that the shadow side of Indian spirituality emerged with it. This odd paradox, that virtues come paired with vices, led Gandhi to the recognition that self-criticism, penance, and reconciliation formed the backbone of any people's movement, and that the masses could only achieve reform by suffering for their own highest ethical aspirations.

These views are postmodern in that they are based upon the anti-foundational epistemology of the mystic "unground" of spiritual religion. Moreover they affirm what I have been calling "the deep self"— not by transcendentalizing the subject, but by regarding it as an historical fiction contained by a larger cosmic identity existing outside the sphere of the mind. Gandhi saw all human values systems as very crude approximations of divinely ordained responsibilities that we must grow into to understand. Nonviolence is an empirical approach to life, not a simplistic moral formula. Nonviolent noncooperation with evil, as a first principle, makes bad faith difficult because it confronts us at every turn with our own limitations and hypocrisies. It is not a panacea for resolving conflicts but a propaedeutic to existential knowledge of ourselves as social beings in a modern context. And God's will, in so far as one can fathom it through direct action in the world, turns out to be multidimensional, complex, novelistic. It unfolds to our degree of understanding and to the extent of our imaginative and empathetic capacities. It forever surprizes, confounds, and challenges. It is as dialogic and as nonviolent as direct action itself. Gandhi remarks:

> There is no such thing as "Gandhism" and I do not want to leave any sect after me. I do not claim to have originated any new principle or doctrine. I have simply tried in my own way to apply the eternal truths to our daily life and problems. . .The opinions I have formed and the conclusions I have arrived at are not final, I may change them tomorrow. Those who believe in the simple truths I have laid down can propagate them only by living them.[19]

Last summer while reading *Zorba the Greek* (about another arch-plebeian), I came across an analogy that illustrates wonderfully the nature of nonviolence and the reason why so many critics miss Gandhi's point by mythologizing his aims and overspiritualizing his doctrines. Early in the book Zorba is explaining to the "book-worm" narrator that playing the santuri is the way he responds to the conflicts in his life. Our narrator, an archtheorist, remarks, "You played to forget your cares, did you?" To which Zorba replies, "I can see you have never played an instrument, Boss."[20] Playing a musical instrument, he explains, requires all your concentration; it is a passion, a struggle. It is a "comfort" only to someone looking at it from the outside. Those who practice the art know its pains, its problematics. It is not a comfort; it is a necessity, a love, a way to transcend. So it is with nonviolence. For Gandhi it is not a doctrine or a panacea so much as a fate, a wager, a passionate commitment, a destiny.

Gandhi's practical perspective was by no means anti-intellectual. In a very real sense Gandhi was a practitioner of the liberal arts, not as the master of a particular set of texts but as the seeker of an inclusive quality of mind and greatness of soul. His contribution to world culture was as much a development of traditional Western values as it was a rejection of its contemporary institutions. His movement was a return to the humanism of his folk culture and the spirituality of his religion through the literariness of the scriptures. Because they were poetic texts, Gandhi could read them as symbolically charged with contemporary meaning, and satyagraha itself is an act of poesis, and act of making, more invention than technique.

If the Buddha offered freedom from suffering through nonattachment, Gandhi offers lessons in nonattachment through creative suffering. Nirvana is not nirvana if it is not shared. The quest for peace of mind must not shut us off from others but open us up to them. Carl Jung once remarked that "neurosis is always a substitute for legitimate suffering."[21] Gandhi inverts the idea to assert that legitimate suffering can be an antidote to political neurosis. The inner and outter battles are the same. Since we all must suffer anyway, the conscious suffering of ahimsa provides us with a way to give that suffering value by transforming life's problems into the very material of personal and public self-perfection.

Gandhi offers us a different kind of heroics—not the epic conceit of martyrdom, but the existential heroics of the inward turn. Rather than educating the will to achieve its desires, he advocates freeing the nervous system to be present to one's painful circumstances. If you can simply experience things as they are without resorting to emotional protections, evasions, violence, or willful rebellion, then the quality of your actions (even if you are doing no more than practicing your religion) will change—and with this qualitative change of being, your relationships with others will also change, altering the system of oppression within which you and your enemy are bound. Nonviolence is, in this sense, the breaking of the circuit of codependency through the practice of virtue and trust.

Eknath Easwaran tells the story of a woman who came to Gandhi to ask if he would tell her child not to eat sugar. The child would eat nothing else. Gandhi told her to come back next week. The following week the woman returned, and Gandhi talked and joked with the boy telling him he really should not eat sugar. After the conversation the woman thanked Gandhi, and then asked him why he had waited a week before speaking to the boy. Gandhi replied, "Last week I too was eating sugar."[22] The point here is not that one should be blameless before others, nor is it merely that one should practice what one preaches. The point is that certain opinions and moral ideas must be earned before we can express them with honest conviction. And they can only be earned by a honest grappling with our own tendencies toward sin and self aggrandizement. Our efforts at self-transformation fail so often because we try to change our exteriors—our bodies, our actions, our behavior, what we say—in hopes of changing others' responses to us. But by changing who we are, we change everything else about us in an instant. This is why prayer, meditation, and the spiritual disciplines of fasting and penance are so important to the nonviolent warrior. They bear in on the problem of our being, rather than projecting blame, and hence power onto other people.

Gandhi's nonviolence rejects the stoic acceptance of the absurd and instead advocates sharing one's vulnerability and fallibility with others. Gandhi's method was built upon making the irrationality of suffering visible, the pain of injustice palpable. He wanted to make grief obvious and our responsibility for it inescapable. The heroism of Gandhi's nonviolent warriors did did not come from their capacity to transcend pain, but from their ability to accept it, acknowledge it, and make something good out of it—from their capacity to "eat" the shadow of imperialist oppression and injustice.

The idea of nonviolent resistance, like "the self-limiting revolution" of Poland's Solidarity union, is *essentially* plebeian because only ordinary people faced every day with their own failures and limitations could have set limits to the amount of power they could ever wish for themselves. Most postmodern plebeian leaders, certainly all of the ones examined in this book, feel a responsibility to temper their own existential projects. Most feel that they have been called by something larger than themselves—a destiny, an historical responsibility, a debt of gratitude to a sacred tradition far greater than their own personal virtue and even greater than their own political cause. Their lives are not their own. And so their actions are bound by certain divine obligations. But these obligations nevertheless assure one of victory since nothing can thwart the divine will—not even failure, suffering, and disaster.

This built-in reassurance creates in religious plebeians an unshakable confidence since the good they sacrifice for is not a fragile historical project that may or may not succeed, but an unshakable transhistorical Reality that transcends their own personal understanding and so cannot be undone by their own failures in service to it. No effort on God's behalf is ever wasted—not because practical achievements always result from them, but because in the end history is absorbed into the eternal, and so the time is always ripe for the good, true, and the beautiful. Nonviolent truth force, in this sense, is an end in itself: plebeian perfection.

CHAPTER THREE

Solzhenitsyn: The God beyond the God that Failed

> *The correct response to modernity is not to place*
> *God beyond the limits of reason, or drag him into*
> *history from the outside, or domesticate him in*
> *"religious sentiment," or bottle him up in bourgeois*
> *mentality by making belief in him a human*
> *excellence. Nor is it the answer to assert that to*
> *move away from him is the destruction of the root*
> *of all human culture. Nor, finally, is the answer to*
> *make of him the object of a free personal decision.*
> *God in Christ is a God suffering, and to share his*
> *weakness is to believe in him. This is what it means*
> *to be a Christian.*
>
> —GUSTAVO GUTIERREZ[1]

Solzhenitsyn's *Gulag Archipelago* has been celebrated as a refutation of Marxism, a revision of Soviet political history, a warning to the West, even a tour de force of literary realism. And yet it is as a moralist that Solzhenitsyn may have contributed most to the thought of our time, for through his sufferings in the camps, he has come upon an aesthetic that recoups the traditional Christian verities on the *other side* of literary modernism. In his articulation of the struggle of concentration camp prisoners to survive physically and spiritually, we see the beginnings of a plebeian postmodernism articulated in prophetic language that challenges all the modernist clichés dominating our age.

One way to see his philosophical contribution is to read the *Gulag* as the antitext to Sartre's *Critique of Dialectical Reason*. This may seem a peculiar way to proceed, for admittedly, Sartre's text is itself eccentric. Yet Sartre's *Critique* does represent, with a fullness and systematic purity shared by few other works, the sweep and the power of what has now come to be called "the hermeneutics of suspicion."[2] His work epitomizes a peculiarly modern way of dealing with moral problems: debunk, deconstruct, and dissolve them by showing how they are products of sociological pressures and ideological mystifications. Solzhenitsyn's *Gulag* is the antithesis to this form of moral reasoning. He debunks, deconstructs, and dissolves the hermeneutics of suspicion by demonstrating how its assumptions lead to a misreading of the empirical realities of history. Then he goes beyond this deconstruction to found a postmodern ethic that affirms human dignity in the face of state terrorism.

The two works treat the same philosophical problems in opposite ways. Like the *Gulag*, Sartre's *Critique* is an encyclopedic work that examines the foundations of social order. And like the *Gulag*, Sartre's critique attempts to think beyond cultural relativism to a new ethic based upon a new philosophic anthropology. But whereas Sartre's work seeks a sophisticated aesthetic frame from which to revolutionize human experience by seeing through class distortions, Solzhenitsyn's work takes such sweeping dialectics to task as symptomatic of the modern predilection to reduction through abstraction. Unlike many contemporary structuralist and deconstructionist thinkers, he does not move behind Sartre's Marxism to expose its disguised conventions. Instead he reports the perspectives of those individuals in the camps who have resisted the triumph of dialectical thinking as it is embodied in the Soviet state philosophy. Thus, Solzhenitsyn's work presents a plurality of views on the metaphysical hegemony embodied in the Soviet system. But more than that, Solzhenitsyn argues that the general overview—born from this witness—is of a higher logical type than dialectics because it contains more "reality." That is to say, it is more inclusive and offers a more compelling explanation of how the world really works. Unlike the modernist sensibility, this higher empiricism is available to everyone. It is not built upon sophisticated class or aesthetic discriminations but upon our common capacity to experience evil and "react to the intolerable."[3]

Both Sartre and Solzhenitsyn start from the assumption that Marxism is the philosophy of our age, but each sees quite different reasons for this. For Sartre, Marxism provides the most reasonable framework from which to articulate a universal history. He admits that it lacks a coherent theory of human subjectivity, but his *Critique* is designed to help correct this limitation. For Solzhenitsyn, Marxism is also the philosophy of our time because it, unlike most other modern philosophical schools, has remained true to the Enlightenment quest for a universal history. Fidelity to this quest provides a context within which modern humanity can work out its own self-definition. But according to Solzhenitsyn, this quest is also tragically flawed. The idea of a universal historical perspective leads to a totalizing role for philosophy. Therefore, built into any search for a world-historical philosophical order are the seeds of a secular state religion. Georg Lukács's claim that dialectical materialism is the culmination of Western humanism would strike Solzhenitsyn as all too true, for dialectical materialism makes explicit the anthropocentric quest by post-Enlightenment thinkers to remake the world over in their own false self-image as creatures of reason. Thus Solzhenitsyn believes that to remain intellectually honest, humanity must find some way of understanding its place in history without basing that understanding upon any world-historical absolutes. In other words, we must seek to order history without letting history itself order us.

To show how this might be done, Solzhenitsyn attempts to rewrite the history of the Russian people from the point of view of those banished from it—the political prisoners and victims of the totalitarian state. He discovers in the process that such a counterhistory is possible only as literature. Or to put it in more contemporary language, literariness became his counter to dialectical reason. He tells the stories of hundreds of individual lives in order to bring home the complex meaning of what had taken place in a way that outstrips any ideological explanation. He explains his "polyphonic" form this way: "Each person becomes the chief character when the action concerns him. This is not just a technique, it is a creed. The narrative focuses on the only human element in existence, the human individual."[4] And what centers all these individual stories is mankind's capacity for fellow feeling, what Solzhenitsyn calls the "solidarity of solitudes." This solidarity, by its mere expression, supplies its own critique of dialectical reason and offers a kind of counter-totalization limited by strict historical veracity and personal eye-witness testimony.

We see this perspective carried through in Solzhenitsyn's magnum opus *The Red Wheel* where he rewrites the history of the Russian Revolution by dividing events up into what he calls "knots." These knots serve as the focus of each succeeding volume in this multivolume history. Knots are crucial units of time in which all the conflicting forces of history stand out in vivid relief in the lives of particular individuals.

Sartre's *Critique*, on the other hand, is essentially modernist. Following Pound's dicta "Make it new," he refurbishes Marxism from the inside—exploding its formal categories while recuperating its aims. He seeks a new formulation of an old program, a more experiential definition of a familiar revolutionary project. He seeks to challenge the postmodern rejection of dialectics in the name of facts and history by demonstrating that these too are creations of human praxis—that there is nothing given to human experience outside the historical struggles that invest them with value. Solzhenitsyn, by contrast, has given up seeking the theoretical high-ground from which to build a

new philosophical system and instead articulates a strategy of resistance against any and all meta-perspectives. When Sartre asks the
question: Can there be any ethical action in a world divided by class?,
Solzhenitsyn asks: Can there be any ethical action in a world domi-
nated by a global philosophy? While Sartre ponders the fate of ethics if
revolution fails to eliminate class distinctions, Solzhenitsyn ponders
the fate of ethics if the revolution succeeds. Sartre's "theory of ensem-
bles," so deftly spelled out in the *Critique*, reflects the radically determined historicity of perception and meaning; whereas, Solzhenitsyn's
Gulag embodies the search for an ethics after history has been seen
through as a power play. In this sense, Solzhenitsyn's work, like all
plebeian postmodernism, parallels the thought before history (myth)
and the thought outside of history (mysticism)—and yet it is neither,
because its main concern is with particular, concrete events in all their
manifest historicity. In other words, Solzhenitsyn's work is based upon
what life experiences have done to him and his ideas—how he has
been delivered from a theoretically tainted view of the world to a more
direct perception of the truth. In short, how suffering made him into an
artist and how art, in turn, made him into a human being.

In a rather harsh critique of Solzhenitsyn's work, the American
novelist William Gass characterized his prose as "twaddle," remarking
that "those who fail as artists pose as prophets."[5] This remark not only
oversimplifies the relationship between art and prophecy (they need
not, after all, be mutually exclusive categories), but typifies a common
misreading of the *Gulag* as primarily ideological. What sustains prophetic art—and one sees this in works such as *Leaves of Grass* and the
book of Isaiah—is the persona of the narrator. In Whitman's case it was
the magnanimous democratic man that sustains and informs the poetry; in Isaiah's case it was the voice of moral indignation. In Solzhenitsyn's case it is the persona of the survivor gifted with a second innocence who sees the world from the other side of history freed from the
petty progressive notions of his age. Impervious to the glamour of evil,
he is constantly astonished by the capacity of individuals (himself in-
cluded) to betray their own humanity. It is the creation of this voice, of
this self, that is both Solzhenitsyn's literary and moral achievement and
the reason why critics have such a difficult time separating his literary
stature from his biography. He has created one out of the other in a
prophetic transformation of his life into parable and protest. Solzhenitsyn, like Whitman, may be his own greatest creation.

Now, admittedly one can find ideological implications here, but
they are derivative, not primary, and the central focus of the *Gulag* as a
work of art is the dramatization of Solzhenitsyn's own spiritual transformation from a status quo Marxist with commonplace literary ambitions

to the chronicler of those ordinary brave men and women banished from history. The *Gulag* represents the eyes and hears of a new spiritual worldview, forged in the Soviet labor camps, that is at once both the form and the content of Solzhenitsyn's story.

Solzhenitsyn begins the *Gulag* with an apology, to all those who did not survive the camps, for not having seen it all nor remembered it all nor divined it all. And then he goes on to admit he did not write the book alone but compiled it from memoirs and letters of 227 witnesses whose names, for security reasons, he could not list. He is speaking for a lost generation, an outcast counterculture, the silenced opposition to what he once was and to what his country had become. Looking back on his own arrest, he asks himself why—after he had seen the inside of the camps—did he keep silent during those few days before his official imprisonment? Why did he not tell someone what he had seen? Why didn't he shout out something in Minsk Station? He answers: he simply did not know what to say; besides only revolutionaries have slogans ready-to-hand, while peaceable average people have no such slogans because their experiences are too complex to be expressed by them. And so Solzhenitsyn says nothing—he waits, bides his time—and seeks a larger audience, posterity itself.

The authority for Sartre's work, on the other hand, derives from such modernist verities as the power, genius, and virtuosity of his system. Its capacity to be internally coherent and self-justified. Its ability to illuminate experience and serve as a strategic intervention into the politics of our time. Thus while Sartre attempts to explain the mechanisms of dialectical reasoning in its social context, Solzhenitsyn's *Gulag* sets a limit to dialectical thought by demonstrating its ultimate moral failure. Unlike Beckett or Borges, who provide modernist critiques of the same kind of dialectical hubris by parodying the infinite regress of its logic but never going beyond that logic themselves, Solzhenitsyn claims to know how to move beyond the absurdities born of an unbridled rationalism, on the grounds that he, and the rest of his fellow zeks, have suffered dialectic's most extreme miscalculation. In the gulag, the dialectical imagination was given power to bend and shape not only literary form but society itself. In this grand construct— the Soviet state—the excesses and amorality of the ideological imagination were revealed.

In contrast to the European avant-garde, of which Sartre was once a leader, Solzhenitsyn does not seek out the "cutting edge" of thought as a way of situating himself intellectually. After all, the latest aesthetic journals seldom make their way inside the gulag. Instead he looks to the actions and beliefs of the "ordinary brave man's" resistance to the state philosophers in order to learn for himself what progressive values are. Marxism, according to Solzhenitsyn, blinds man to authentic moral illumination because, like many other modern aesthetics, it values experience primarily as food for theory, and it values theory primarily as a means to progress. Such thinking does not value life as an end in itself, nor can it appease humanity's irrational will—what Sartre might call its "thrownness." This will, Solzhenitsyn argues, cannot find happiness serving any abstraction, even one so grandiose as heaven on earth. Marxism only links the individual's personal ambitions to a global drama, and so inflates the individual's own neurosis under the cover of moral perfection.

But—and here is the surprising truth revealed to Solzhenitsyn in the camps—you can harness the will through exactly the reverse process. You can have the worldly significance of everything you do taken away. You can have your pride and your future annihilated. You can become ahistorical and politically anonymous—erased from society by the powers that be. When this happens, your will is no longer fueled by personal ambition or the demands of the historical moment. Instead, if you survive, you become a quiet, solitary resistance fighter, combating that evil within everyone that wants to subject life to its own tedious projects. Solzhenitsyn even blesses his prison cell for having purged him of the confusions of his age, for once on the other side of history, free from the petty progressive notions of one's time, one enters history in a new way, as a witness to the force within that intuitively resists oppression born of the human will to power.

Suffering has cracked even modernism's amorphous and expandable shell. We suffer not only because our world is too small but also because our forms of expression are too thin. Life demands more than we expect; it doesn't fit our forms, our dialectical schemes, or our aesthetic systems. It uproots, breaks, and smashes us. Dying, we are forced to grow, to grow beyond such toys as metacriticism and metaphilosophy to something else: something simple, direct, and accurate—our own pain. As we suffer, we cling all the more tightly to things that transcend death, the spiritual ideals of meaning and purpose.

Not that Solzhenitsyn celebrates suffering as a good in itself; he merely appreciates its purging effects. The message is that we will not, maybe even cannot, truly attend to the world free from petty self-seeking until all our illusions and ambitions are stripped away. Once we give up, or are forced to give up, our pride, we acquire a strange new fearlessness, and life partakes of a new presence or grace. This new presence can make us brave, and bravery even more than theoretical acumen is the antidote to oppression, because acts of bravery lead to new perceptions; whereas acts of shrewdness, even when they are subject to correction, lead only to new tactics and so cannot adjust themselves with respect to their essential aims or lead to any radically new empirical discoveries about the world.

The modernist literary avant-garde chose exile as the price one had to pay for artistic integrity and freedom. Solzhenitsyn, like his fellow zeks, was thrown out of society by force of arms, and so his aesthetic is fugitive in a new way: it is popular. That is to say, the bohemianism of most European movements registers a conscious rejection of modern bourgeois civilization and, hence, searches for new aesthetic frames of reference intentionally foreign to common experience. But Solzhenitsyn seeks to defend the common man against the power of an enthroned and politically enforced modernism—dialectical materialism—and so he seeks aesthetic frames of reference capable of winning back common sense, shared humanity, and the solidarity of solitudes. It is as if being common, modernism sought the strange; whereas being estranged, Solzhenitsyn and his plebeian comrades seek the common. Of course, this was impossible for them, so their works take on that peculiar postmodern blending (or pastiche) that juxtapositions internally coherent subcultures against mainstream modernist chaos and places the private but profound insight within the transnational clichés of an increasingly hegemonic world system.

It is in the contrasts Solzhenitsyn provides us between his zek sensibility and the modern world that the plebeian mentality stands most revealed. He writes, for example, of his speech at the Nobel Prize dinner in which he was given three minutes to address the plight of the victims of Soviet state terrorism while his audience consumed a sumptuous gourmet dinner.

> (Gentlemen—your Scythian guest is disappointed in you: Why all those lambs-wool hairdos under the arc lights? Why is a white tie de rigueur and a camp jerkin not allowed? And what strange custom is this—to listen to the speech in which a laureate sums up his work, his whole life, with food before you? How abundantly the tables are laden, how sumptuous are the dishes, how casually you pass them, as though you saw them every day. Serve yourselves, chew your food, wash it down. . . but what of the writing on the wall, in letters of fire:—"Mene, mene, tekel, upharsin." Do you not see it . . . ?)
>
> "Well, then, let us not forget at this festive table that this very day, political prisoners are holding a hunger strike in defense of rights curtailed or trampled under foot."[6]

He fills the *Gulag* with one concrete event like this after another; each one illustrating even more dramatic contrasts. And although these stories do not mesh into any single plot in a traditional Aristotelian sense, collectively they evoke a pattern—the polyphonic pattern of a symphony of moral outrages. Each one is a unique note and testimony to the many faces of oppression, to the many modes of moral and spiritual resistance, and to the many brave men and women who died standing up to the tryanny of an empowered dialectical scheme.

By contrast, Sartre's text is a cathedral of coined abstractions and stipulative definitions. His sentences turn themselves inside out to express the most subtle turns of reflection upon reflection. The search is for the most inclusive, and therefore most theoretical, generalization. It is the rhetoric of a policy maker or administrator.

Sartre's work embodies the modernist notion that the thinker must stand outside the immediacy of life and view it from invented aesthetic frames which remake, renew, and redeem it from bourgeois existence. Solzhenitsyn's work, on the other hand, embodies the capacity of the artist to stand in the shoes of others. Where Sartre seeks to recoup humanism through a methodology that allows him to debunk any competing ideology, Solzhenitsyn seeks to recoup human integrity by attending to the particulars of human history as part of a larger, if hidden, spiritual drama. This drama, however, is not the premodern story of a humanity redeemed by the Church but the postmodern drama of a humanity whose redemption is still in the balance. Strange as it may seem, on this point Solzhenitsyn is the more existential of the two thinkers. He admits, for example, that we do not yet really know what grief or happiness *are*. Both works contain glossarys. Sartre's is a listing of all his invented terms and their relationships to one another; Solzhenitsyn's is a list of names.

The philosophical foundation of Solzhentisyn's Christianity rests upon the plebeian's mythopoetic conception of religion as the practice of virtue (as opposed to Sartre's modernist conception of religion as a kind of mystified ideology). Plebeians, like primitives, believe in transcendence as a way of making sense out of their own resistance to the ways of the world—not as a means for justifying their privileges, indulging in the irrational, or dismissing contemporary problems. For plebeians, beliefs are survival techniques (necessities), and the incredible premise of a prime mover is their trump card against all the power brokers and social Darwinists of this world who would define them in terms of their own projects and ambitions.

This is why Solzhenitsyn finds the inspiration for his postmodernism in the zek of the gulag and not in the modernist masters in the West. For the modernists, in creating their new mythologies, did not begin with the plebeian's incredible premise of a divine order behind the flux of experience. Instead they moved further into the flux itself in order to further destabilize the already tottering status quo. For Solzhenitsyn, such a strategy played into the hands of the state philosophers and proved too thin to deal meaningfully with the reality of the camps and the triumph of dialectics. The magnitude of the suffering demanded an aesthetic which could somehow break through both the intellectual impotence of the dying order and the reductionism of the ascending methodologies. What was needed was a new expression of moral presence. Someone had to testify to the reality of something outside dialectical redefinition in order to create a handle with which we could pull free from the ascendent nihilism.

In the camps, Solzhenitsyn discovered the absolute upon which to found this moral presence: the sanctity of individual conscience. But unlike premodern times, integrity of person was no longer a birthright, and it could not be assumed that it was possessed by every mortal soul. In Solzhenitsyn's postmodern world, integrity was something that had to be won back, earned, recreated. The experience of the camps brought this shocking truth home to him. Just as Heidegger argued that the real problem of modernity is not that we have forgotten the question of Being but that we have forgotten that we have forgotten the question of Being, Solzhenitsyn comes to the equally startling conclusion that not only have moderns lost their moral center, but they have lost their awareness that they have lost their moral center. In other words, amorality has been established through the triumph of dialectics as a form of higher consciousness, when in fact it represents the triumph of the will to power over the intellectual conscience. In the West many critics assume modernism to have triumphed over the positivisms of the early twentieth century. But modernism itself may simply be another manifestation of the positivist desire to conquer life via theory—only now theory masks itself as art.

For Solzhenitsyn moral reasoning can be won back only by those forced through their suffering to perceive the lie. And the lie, from his point of view, is the modernist conceit that forms and ideas, not people, are the ultimate reality. Both dialecticians and modernists like Sartre possess a misguided commitment to formal principles in a world in which ideas are at best tools, at worst, traps. Solzhenitsyn respects and uses ideas to further truth, which for him must always remain beyond ideas and, therefore, forever outside any philosophical regime. For Sartre, thinking is the way one grounds the ideal in the real. And though he would never put it so crudely, thought as theory is his true absolute. It explains power to him, regulates his actions, and dictates morality. The *Gulag* in its rhetoric and in its themes attempts to refute this presumption, and to the extent it succeeds, it is postmodern.

But if the *Gulag* is the antitext to Satre's *Critique*, it is also the sister text to Kafka's *The Trial*. Both begin with arrests and follow through, in painstaking detail, the logical and psychological consequences that follow. In both the law stands over and above individuals with a radiance and power its petty representatives lack. There is an absurd contrast between the system and the people who inhabit it—an astounding, even shocking, incommensurability between individual aspirations, fears, and capacities and the structures within which they must operate.

The great difference, of course, is that Kafka's work operates as an endlessly decipherable, universal fable of the modern; whereas, the *Gulag* is much more historically contextualized, consciously limited, particular. The law Solzhenitsyn examines is not anything so sweeping as "THE LAW" Kafka is concerned with—but an historically constituted penal system that can be situated precisely in chronological time. Its origins are traced, its power mechanisms analyzed, its effects described. Thus, Solzhenitsyn's literary experiment brings Kafka's nightmare down to cases. Where Kafka resists any temptation to make literal an authorial point of view for the sake of propounding the spiritual depth and complexity of his work, Solzhenitsyn makes it his conscious project to expose the literal nightmare of the Soviet dialectical fantasy.

The other big difference is that K is an individual; whereas, Solzhenitsyn's zek is a collective being born into solidarity with other oppressed people. Admittedly, Solzhenitsyn's polyphonic strategies mitigate this somewhat, but every character in the *Gulag* is understood in relationship to others, in their capacity to be-for-others, in their ethical identities. Kafka explores the psychological depths; Solzhenitsyn the social conscience. Solzhenitsyn's plebeianism exchanges the angst of the alienated modern for the survival imperatives of an embattled people. K is alone. His inner life defines his world. The zek looks outward again, and although from Kafka's perspective this may be a spiritual evasion of sorts, it is nevertheless one way to survive the horror of the modern. If Kafka is finally our most courageous modernist explorer, the Solzhenitsyn of the *Gulag* is his prudent, postmodern double who prefers not to gaze too long into the abyss lest the abyss gaze back at him. He turns to those around him and imagines a life of solidarity latent in the fallen world.

In a moving passage toward the end of the first volume of the *Gulag*, Solzhenitsyn tells of the time he was sitting on a bench between two KGB guards in a train depot. His transfers to new camps were the only times he was among free people. As he sat there, he reflected upon the petty concerns of people around him and how he longed to tell them the truth.

And how do you bring it home to them? By an inspiration? By a vision? A dream? Brothers! People! Why has life been given you? In the deep, deaf stillness of midnight, the doors of the death cells are being swung open—and the great-souled people are being dragged out to be shot.[7]

But then Solzhenitsyn answers his own question. And to our surprise it is free from anger and resentment.

If you want I'll spell it out for you right now. Do not pursue what is illusory—property and position: all that is gained at the expense of your nerves decade after decade, and is confiscated in one fell night. Live with a steady superiority over life—don't be afraid of misfortune and do not yearn for happiness; it is after all, all the same: the bitter never lasts forever, and the sweet never fills the cup to overflowing.[8]

Such a remark may strike a neo-Marxist like Sartre as stoic, but Solzhenitsyn goes beyond resignation to an absolute identification with his enemies that transforms his heroic resistance into compassion, wisdom, and the ultimate redeeming action—art. He continues:

Rub your eyes and purify your heart—and prize above all else in the world those who love you and wish you well. Do not hurt them or scold them, and never part with them in anger; after all you simply do not know: it might be the last act before your arrest. . . But the convoy guards stroke the black handles of the pistols in their pockets. And we sit there, three in a row, sober fellows, quiet friends.[9]

Solzhenitsyn does not refute the system that imprisoned him; he utterly destroys its authority from within through an act of moral courage and spiritual witness. It is as a writer that Solzhenitsyn defeats the gulag. And although he is quick to point out that words are not enough to defeat injustice, his book and its worldwide impact make clear that authentic human expression can change the way the world sees itself and thereby change the world.

For Solzhenitsyn, words can still escape the relations of power and, in Foucault's phrase, acquire "an inverse energy—a discharge" against the prevailing "regime of truth" (which in this case is not truth at all, but a lie).[10] Such revolutionary speech is spoken one-to-one, between solitudes. Its source is individual souls—specific, breathing, working, loving, suffering people. But today's world driven by the notion that reality is produced by theory and that theory is proved by the number of people that believe it, doesn't take the individual seriously unless he or she can speak his or her truth through art: the one institution in this abstract and statistical age still capable of expressing the universality and importance of personal experience. And so, for Solzhenitsyn, the artist has an important role to play—not as the antenna of his or her race, but as its moral ground.

Solzhenitsyn's work represents a renewed respect for the native wisdom of indigenous peoples—natives and peasants. Their perspective on life is outside of history and yet forever contemporary because it is not so much an ideology as a kind of intelligence. *Phronesis* is the best Greek equivalent; *know-how* is the American coinage. Yet neither word really captures the totality of life that such a direct, simple, feeling-based existence embraces. It is a kind of wisdom-skill born from direct contact with the earth and with the act of creation. It is practical wisdom in the same sense in which the great religions of the world are practical: its aim is to show us the way through this world to that which transcends it—genius, heroism, sainthood. The American poet Gary Snyder points out the timeless witness of the "old ways" in this account of the education of a Papago poet:

> At very bottom the question is "how do you prepare your mind to become a singer?" . . . An attitude of openness, inwardness, gratitude; plus meditation, fasting, a little suffering, some rupturing of the day-to-day ties with the social fabric. I quote again from the Papago: "A man who desires song did not put his mind on words and tunes. He put it on pleasing the supernaturals. He must be a good hunter or a good warrior. Perhaps they would like his ways. And one day in natural sleep he would hear singing. . . . Perhaps the clouds sing or the wind or the feathery red rain spider on its invisible rope. The reward of heroism is not personal glory nor riches. The reward is dreams."[11]

Here we see Solzhenitsyn's most fevered intuition affirmed: art is nothing if it is not born of moral virtue. To be worthy of songs, heroism is required. Not the heroism of daring exploits, necessarily, but the heroism of sacrifice and the acceptance of suffering for something greater than oneself. Those quiet acts of duty make insights possible, condense the psyche, and thereby lend authority to one's voice.

Solzhenitsyn reflects upon the time shortly after his release from the cancer ward when he heard advice to young writers broadcast over Soviet radio. By that time he had already written *The First Circle* and the short story "Shch–854" and had composed thousands of lines of poetry in the camps, by memory, without the aid of pen or paper. Yet here were official Soviet "success stories" explaining the need writers have for a nice environment, pleasant stimuli, peace and quiet—all the accoutrements necessary to produce unconsciously compromised art. Solzhenitsyn remarks:

> I myself had learned long ago in the camp to compose and write as I marched in a column under escort; out on the frozen steppe; in an iron foundry. . . The shrill, vainglorious literature of the establishment—with its dozen fat magazines, its two literary newspapers, its innumerable anthologies, its novels between hard covers, its collected works, its annual prizes. . . I had once and for all recognized as unreal, and I did not waste my time or exasperate myself by trying to keep up with it. I knew without looking that there could be nothing of merit in all this. Not because no talent could emerge there—no doubt it sometimes did, but there it perished too. For it was a barren field, that which they sowed.[12]

And why was this field barren? It was barren because in buying into the premises of socialist realism—the established Soviet school—one denied the authenticity of one's own experience and the original community from which one's plebeian soul had emerged. And so no matter how skilled one was as a stylist, one could never defeat the lie or tell the truth. For Solzhenitsyn art enters history as that which stands counter to the official history, as a questioning and refutation of the philosophical truisms of the age.

His aesthetic goals are made explicit in his advice to young writers. 1) Avoid superficial political satire 2) There is no need to look for new forms: develop a feeling for your native soil, your native history—all this will provide more than enough material, and the material itself will dictate the form. 3) The goal is unforced, organic imagery springing directly from the life of the people.[13]

The *Gulag Archipelago* is the story of the education of a plebeian who sheds his status quo Marxism which was, in fact, a reductionist plebeian misreading of Marxist commonplaces, to become a fully self-conscious plebeian rebel identified with his own resisting subculture. It is a conversion story, depicting zek life from the inside: how they feel toward nature, the regime, the hypocrisies, and the everyday conceits of Soviet life. Solzhenitsyn remarks, "As soon as you have renounced that aim of 'surviving at any price,' and gone where the calm and simple people go—then imprisonment begins to transform your character in an astonishing way."[14] He sees for the first time that good and evil are not sociological categories but contend at the center of each and every heart. And that his heart had been occupied, just like his country, with an alien metaphysic, empowered by a political regime, that had blinded him not only to his own best self, but to his moral responsibilities. In the camps, he wakes up. He finds a nation within a nation, and a God beyond the God that failed. And he dedicates himself to becoming the prophetic voice and the personal embodiment of this new dispensation.

CHAPTER FOUR

Wiesel: The Idea of the People after the Holocaust

> *Sartre used to say that human beings are*
> *condemned to be free. I would paraphrase that and*
> *say, we are condemned to save the world with our*
> *memories. The question is: How? In other words,*
> *how do we manage to humanize destiny?*
>
> —ELIE WIESEL[1]

The Old Testament Hebrews are one of the most perfect examples of the plebeian mentality. In the Torah they are chosen to represent humanity before God. They are a people whose peculiar story self-consciously represents the story of every other people. This is an odd identity, to say the least, since it defines one's uniqueness as one's special responsibility to *be universal*. Ironically, however, one's access to the universal is acquired by remaining true to one's sectarian origins—to one's particular indigenous culture, to the inherent "strangeness" of one's own historical experience. The message here seems to be that what is essentially human is not the literal events one undergoes, but the need to humanize them.

Thus, God enters the history of the Hebrews—as God enters into the history of all peoples—in order to turn it into literature and parable, into a metaphoric vehicle in search of an inscrutable tenor. Gandhi's sense that Western history is an interruption of an eternally present Nature is confirmed in the Biblical understanding of human time as contained between Genesis and apocalypse—in the messianic conceit that history is fallen time, and narrative the aperture through which it is overcome as mere event and transformed into meaning. In this sense, Hebrew scripture offers a way out of the nightmare of history by transforming history into the narrative of the self's overcoming of the world. Its purpose is to untie individuals from determinisms, invoke freedom, and refigure historical experience as lesson, drama, poem.

So although it would be true to say that Judaism is a faith that is centered on a people, no one could ever call it a populist religion, because its essence resides in its literariness and in its invocation of law as a counter to the unlimited play of desire across time. And although the Pentateuch and the prophets offer a politics keyed to liberation, service to the poor, and resistance to oppression,[2] its categories pre-date the Enlightenment, and so it does not honor individual liberty as much as perpetual self-criticism in the light of transcendent standards.

Very early in their history, the Hebrews confronted the hubris of nationalism and the absence of God, who fled their temple. These crises seem "modern" today and are the property of many traditions, but the literature of Judaism is built upon these themes and offers us the fruits of three thousand years of reflection on the meaning of life after history has been seen through as a play for power, and after one's "difference" has been reaffirmed as one's essential link to the rest of humanity.

During the Holocaust this ancient plebeian orientation met its modern opposite in the Nazi plague. It was *as a people* that the Jews were singled out, and it was as a people that Germany responded to Hitler's vision of their destiny. In this sense the Holocaust was the ultimate assault upon *the* people of Western civilization and the my-thopoetic sensibility at the core of their identity. In both victim and victimizer, the values of family, ethnicity, national heritage, spir-ituality, and common sense were transformed beyond recognition. The old faiths, the old sentimentalities, childhood, conscience, traditional intimacies—all were gone. They were "made new" in horrific ways, modernized beyond belief. Nazism was a brutal, modern, surreal in-version of plebeian values into a parody of a people. And we who come after can no longer look at these disfigured verities in the same way. We are on the far side of their profanation. And if we try to live the old verities today, invoke the memory of a just God, remember the victo-ries of our people, honor our ancestors or even profess their values, we find ourselves caught up in a myriad of contradictions and self-doubts.

Thus, the writings of Elie Wiesel, as a deep reflection upon the reality of the Holocaust and its significance to our time constitutes one of our most profound meditations on the fate of the plebeian sensibility in the twentieth century. In his works we see a dialogue of the tradi-tional self, the deep self, the religious self, with the modern hubris of nationalism and technology, with evil, genocide, self-negation, and despair. His works are probes, explorations, speculations into what kind of spirituality is possible to us after the impotence of our institu-tional protections against evil have been revealed.

His thoughts on these matters have evolved from the stark realism of *Night* to the holy madness of *Twilight*. But it would be inaccurate to see progress here. The issues he addresses are far too complex and far too ultimate for that. Rather, each stage in his work reflects new facets of the mystery of God's silence and humanity's longing.

What he has been able to accomplish is to bring together a family of concerns not hitherto acknowledged as essentially linked: self-conscious ethnicity as a prelude to full humanity, the Holocaust as ethical turning point, madness as a means to morality, and narrative as *the* medium of ethical communication. These are not separate themes for Wiesel but parts of a seamless web that constitutes a single unified vision of post-Holocaust spirituality.

The essence of this vision is perhaps best illustrated by the fable he tells at the close of *The Town Beyond the Wall.*

> Legend tells us that one day man spoke to God in this wise:
> "Let us change about. You be man, and I will be God. For only one second."
> God smiled and gently asked him, "Aren't you afraid?"
> "No. And You?"
> Nevertheless he granted man's desire. He became a man, and the man took his place and immediately availed himself of his omnipotence: he refused to revert to his previous state. So neither God nor man was ever again what he seemed to be.
> Years passed, centuries, perhaps eternities. And suddenly the drama quickened. The past for one, and the present for the other, were too heavy to be borne.
> As the liberation of one was bound to the liberation of the other, they renewed the ancient dialogue whose echoes come to us in the night, charged with hatred, with remorse, and most of all with infinite yearning.[3]

In this story we see the moral universe turned upside down. This is a description of our age. A Promethean age in which the will has triumphed and the divine has taken on the face of the victim, the sufferer, the outcast. The God in humanity is burdened by the present; the humanity in God by the past. They confront one another through prayer, ritual and prophecy.

To speak out of and through a tradition, one's particular history, is the only way one can be human—there are no acontextual absolutes. And so the renewed dialogue between humanity and God must take place on partisan terms, within specific traditions, in full memory of the past—never forgetting and never betraying those who went before. This fable is a story about the weight of history, not its lightness. About the burden of one's humanity, not one's existential freedom. It is also a story about the suffering of God and about our responsibility before the almighty. It explains God's silence and impotence without demeaning God's character, and calls on humanity to master the arts of humility, service, and self-abnegation.

And yet because this story is legendary, it is a self-conscious fiction, a transparent myth, as much a guess as a sermon or assertion. It isn't *really* the way things are between God and humanity, but it is some of the way things are. And because the genre itself bespeaks the tentative nature of its assertions, it is a more honestly qualified description than even the most circumspect theological claims. There is no dogma or doctrine here; it is all perspective, attitude, and spirit. It announces a liberation theology built upon an ancient dialogue and charged with the infinite longing of the present.

This story would be reenacted again in the closing scenes of Wiesel's novel *Twilight*, where a mad man who thinks he is God is confronted by a man who treats him as if he were God—demanding an explanation for the Holocaust. The man who thinks he is God weeps silently, and the man who accuses him turns in reflection upon his own "mad" act of accusation.

> I immediately regret my words. As I turn toward him, I think I see tears rolling down the side of his face. I tell myself: this suffering is human, not divine. Here is a madman who believes he is God, and here I am, addressing him as if he were. . .[4]

Again what is being played out here is the tragic incommensurability between our need to anthropomorphize God, and God's inability to live up to the resulting moral responsibility. Both ourselves and God suffer in turn, yet both are in a dialogue—however mad—over the meaning and value of creation itself.

One of the most profound experiences of my life as a teacher occurred while I was studying *Night* with a group of fourteen-year-old boys during the Lenten season. As most literature teachers will confess, sometimes when we are trying to explain a work, we are visited by a peculiar eloquence not entirely our own, and the book we are teaching not only teaches itself, but lifts us up to its own heights. I remember specifically the well known scene at the end of the fourth section of *Night* with its chilling description of the hanging of three prisoners— one a young boy who did not immediately die because his body was too light to snap his neck. The other prisoners are forced to march by the corpses and this child's half-dead body. Someone asks, "Where is God now?" And Wiesel hears a voice within answer, "Where is He? Here He is—He is hanging here on the gallows. . ."[5]

The students were puzzled by this line and wanted to know what it meant. Had I known then the fable at the end of *The Town Beyond the Wall*, I might have read it to them. But I didn't. We were alone with the text, alone with the horrific authenticity of this witness, and I was a little self-conscious about presuming to "teach" this book, especially to such callow youth. But I took courage from an account I had read of Wiesel's own appearance before a high school in New York where he answered each and every question posed to him with patience and complete honesty. For example, one of the kids had asked him to describe the look on the faces of the guards as they committed their atrocities. Wiesel answered that he didn't look into their eyes; they were his masters. I could at least try to be as honest about my own experience. Besides, there is something about Wiesel's prose—its honesty—its refusal to protect the reader from the realities of life, however harsh, that immediately earned the trust of these adolescent boys. They felt elevated by his respect for them as readers. Of all of the books we read that year, *Night* was the book they took most seriously. They wanted to talk about it; they needed to talk about it. But they didn't know what to say. I was there, so I talked with them.

"What does that mean, that God is hanging on the gallows?" they asked.

I could have offered some glib remark about the death of God, but I decided to be honest. "I don't know."

"Did it really happened?"

"Yes."

"This is really a wierd book!"

And I could see by their expressions they really meant awesome, uncanny, disturbing. Finally one student ventured his own version of a Catholic interpretation.

"I think he was talking about Jesus. The three men, the suffering one in the middle—it's like Jesus on the cross."

"This is a child," I said. "A million of them were killed by the Nazis. It's not Jesus."

"But it's a Jewish boy. Isn't it a symbol?"

I was uneasy saying no. All literature is in some sense symbolic, since it synthesizes the abstract and the concrete into typical representations, but *Night* was different. It was testimony and witness, an attempt not to betray those who died, and I wanted to live up as best I could to Wiesel's intentions.

"No," I said finally. "It is not a symbol. At least not the kind of symbol we are used to talking about. It would be just as accurate to say Jesus is a symbol for this child than to say that this child is a symbol for Jesus." I could tell by their quizzical faces they weren't getting me. I was sounding heretical. Perhaps even a bit crazy. "Look," I continued. "It's really a question of what constitutes the fuller reality. In this story nothing is more profound than the death of this child—except perhaps the silence of God. I think for Wiesel, Jesus's death does not take precedent over the death of two million Jewish children. And we are meant to experience the whole spiritual, historical, and personal horror of the camps through his precise particularizations. To see this child as a *symbol* would be to forget his humanity—which is to say his precious irreplaceability, his never-again, individual character."

"But then what's it *mean?*" they asked again. "What is it supposed to mean *to us.*"

"The fact that a death like this could happen—did happen—confronts us with certain uncomfortable truths about life and what it means to be a human being, such as the vulnerability of the innocent before those who would be Gods—or at least would be Masters of Life. But there isn't always a universal truth in every situation. Perhaps the revelation here is more particular and temporal. Perhaps that's just the point: that death in the camps was never symbolic, it was always personal, insufferable, beyond mythic explanation."

The class didn't say anything. I wondered whether they followed me. I wondered whether I followed myself. But I could tell they were thinking.

"So you mean that this death doesn't mean anything *good,*" said Richard Valdez straining to make sense of it all. "That its not part of some point he's trying to make, that its a total waste, and *that's* what it means."

"Sort of," I replied. "I don't think it was a *total* waste, because it did affect people, change lives, force us to examine our consciences, but these effects are never to be seen as worth any fraction of the price that was paid for them. This death is not redemptive in any Christian sense; it is one of the worst things that human beings have ever done."

"Even worse than satanic tortures and sexual mutilations," asked Jimmy Coleman. I could tell by this question that the conversation had become quite real for him.

"There were tortures and mutilations in the camps. Besides, this was government-sponsored torture and mutilation aimed at an entire ethnic population, endorsed by 'good' citizens as prudent political policy. In this sense it *was* the worst thing civilized humanity ever did."

"So what can *we* do about it. It's over. Most of these people are dead."

"They live in memory and conscience. Their ghosts haunt our lives. They are as real as we are, maybe even realer," I said.

"How can they be realer than we are?" Jimmy asked.

"They died for who they were. They died because they were Jews. We would do well to stand for so much."

"So the whole book *is* symbolic; the boy's death *is* a symbol," Jimmy insisted.

I attempted one last time to explain the distinction. "No, its a memory. And now, in a way, its our memory, too, so we've got to live with it, and we have to live lives of substance to be worthy of it. If we live, we have obligations as survivors not to betray the humanity of those who came before us by belittling our own."

"But how do you do that? How do you live a life of substance?"

"For a start," I said, "you can read the rest of this book." They laughed and took this as the typical manipulative evasion of an English teacher, but I meant it.

Wiesel, himself, believes that stories can educate, bridge worlds, and humanize fate. He even goes so far as to equate literature with deeds. Narratives invoke, involve and refuse to abstract us from experience. If we refuse their wager, call them lies, or resist their reality by dismissing them as merely fictitious, then we miss them completely. They mean nothing without the reader taking a risk—without the reader entering into the deed as it unfolds on the page.

Reading is more than an ethical act; it is an act of self-creation. Ontological. World-making. And the fact that its mechanisms of operation can be deconstructed and exposed through linguistic analysis does not in itself answer the pressing moral question: How should we read? Wiesel's answer on this is clear: one should read so as to correct injustice.[6] And injustice comes primarily from forgetting, or never having known, the full bill of particulars that constitute the human condition.

Just as Gandhi saw deeds becoming myth, so Wiesel sees myth becoming act. There are other ways than dialectics of finding one's bearings in history. Stories work quite well. But while stories and myths are being unmasked as disguised ideology by contemporary literary theorists, Wiesel responds to the old stories with new ones. He deconstructs, reinterprets, confronts, and demystifies, but not from the relatively safe position of the theorist, but as a contending storyteller himself, as an historically engaged, historically limited and "compromised" creator in his own right, seeking the coherence of his own vision rather than the illusory supremacy of his method. As a storyteller Wiesel is no less sophisticated than those who demystify texts; it is just that he does not share their belief in a nonliterary metalanguage of description capable of administering the Word. Rather one must try to speak, to tell the story, and to tell it again differently, to serve as a messenger so as not to betray the past or humanity. "Whatever I have," he tells us, "I have received. Whatever I give belongs to who knows how many generations of Jewish scholars, and dreamers and poets."[7]

Wiesel is in this sense his own narratologist, in that the tradition within which he works is steeped in a theoretical self-consciousness that runs in a different direction than mainstream Aristotelian poetics, and builds upon the multi-layered prose of the Biblical redactors, the parables of Hasidim and of Kafka, the Talmud's self-references and symbolism, Kabbalah, and Midrash. Aristotle—writing late in Greek history—wrote his poetics as part of the movement toward drama, logos, and democracy and away from ritual, elitism, myth, and aristocracy. He was a student of Sophocles, and his poetic was a contribution to the debate between philosophy and religion, between rationality and tradition. Its purpose was to mediate, synthesize, reconcile, and thereby overcome their opposition. The philosophical aesthetics and practical criticism that issue from his work reconceptualize the practice of art in terms of its beauty and goodness, ignoring its unique status as a process and as an act.

Wiesel's own aesthetic works differently. For him "holy madness" and the art that embodies it do not synthesize the abstract and the concrete into a new category of "the typical" but rather challenge the whole prevailing scheme of categories by which humanity measures the cosmos. Art is a means for momentarily transcending history so that we can redescribe it and make our liberation from it—at least in our imaginations—a fait accompli. To be insane is to reject the given universals, and in so far as those categories are the accepted intellectual currency of the age that produced Auschwitz, holy madness is the only true sanity. The Bible, in this sense, is a mad work—eschewing history for parables, metaphors, the higher reason of the feeling heart. God enters into the lives of the Jews to turn their experiences into literature and lesson. Art is part of the messianic conceit that history is fallen time, and narrative the aperture through which history is overcome as mere event and rendered into meaning. Literature, like Scripture, thus evades positivist history, transforms it, unties it, revokes it, and rereads it.

Wiesel remarks, "We are the imagination and madness of the world—we are imagination gone mad. One has to be mad today to believe in God and in man—one has to be mad to believe. One has to be mad to want to stay human. Be mad, Rabbi, be mad!"[8] The divine madness expresses itself outside of history, outside of power—in the children, the oppressed, the ignored, the prisoner, the victim, the outcast, the remnant.

Given the facts of the Holocaust, humanity and history are irreconcilable. The "Jewish Question" is the question of the impossibility of assimilation of humanity to its circumstance. Wiesel remarks,

> . . . To be a Jew then meant to fight both the complacency of the neutral and the hate of the killers. And to resist—in any way, with any means. And not only with weapons. The Jew who refused death, who refused to believe in death, who chose to marry in the ghetto, to circumcise his son, to teach him the sacred language, to bind him to the threatened and weakened lineage of Israel—that Jew was resisting. The professor or shopkeeper who disregarded facts and warnings and clung to illusion, refusing to admit that people could succumb to degradation—he, too, was resisting. There was no essential difference between the Warsaw ghetto fighters and the old men getting off the train in Treblinka: because they were Jewish, they were all doomed to hate, and death.
>
> In those days, more than ever, to be a Jew signified *refusal*. Above all, it was refusal to see reality and life through the enemy's eyes—a refusal to resemble him, to grant him that victory too.[9]

This is a refusal that does not stop and cannot end.

Wiesel once remarked that the truth is betrayed by repetition. He did not mean that we should not continue telling the story of the Holocaust, but we should be careful to tell it anew each time—not just repeat our words. But how does one keep memory alive without repeating? How can we keep telling the truth about the past without merely saying the same things over and over again and thereby distort them? This is the problem of the educator, the exegist, and the interpreter. For Wiesel it is also the problem of the writer, the priest, the prophet, and the Jew. The answer implied by all Wiesel's works is that the literary imagination is the key to keeping memory alive and truth served—through the idioms of myth, the resonating depths of the image, and the magic of the teaching story. We cannot simply keep repeating the old remembrances; we must continually recontextualize them, or their uncanniness will be lost and their significance fade in cliché.

In his book *Somewhere a Master: Further Hasidic Portraits and Legends*, Wiesel provides his own list—a list of "truths" communicated by a great Jewish teacher—that announce the imperatives of his own postmodern plebeianism.

1. Not to give up—even if some questions are without answers—go on asking them.

2. Doubts are not necessarily destructive—provided they bring one to a Rebbe.

3. One must not think that one is alone and one's tragedy is exclusively one's own; others have gone through the same sorrow and endured the same anguish.

4. One must know where to look, and to whom.

5. God is everywhere, even in pain, even in the search for faith.

6. A good story in Hasidism is not about miracles, but about friendship and hope—the greatest miracles of all.[10]

What is plebeian here is the self-help practicality of this spiritual advice; it is applicable to individual lives and particular problems. What is modern here is the embrace of uncertainty and process. But it is the synthesis of these two orientations that makes Wiesel a plebeian postmodern.

He is able to bridge faith and insecurity—not merely subsume one within the other. And he is able to affirm the questioning heart without giving over to sentimental, bourgeois excess. He is a patient man in an unpatient time, expressing a counsel that heals our urgencies—not so much by diluting them through a long view of things, but by demolishing them from the inside out by exposing their presumptions. This is plebeian postmodernism at its cutting edge. It constitutes an appeal to the simple people to change the course of history—"shorten exile"— by respecting truth, valuing friendship and "accepting the yoke" of heaven.

> . . . to be a Jew is precisely to reveal oneself within one's contradictions by accepting them. It means safeguarding one's past at a time when mankind aspires only to conquer the future; it means observing Shabbat when the offical day of rest is Sunday or Friday; it means fervently exploring the Talmud, with its seemingly antiquated laws and discussions, while outside, not two steps away from the heder or the yeshiva, one's friends and parents are rounded up or beaten in a pogrom; it means asserting the right of spirituality in a world that denies spirituality; it means singing and singing again, louder and louder, when all around everything heralds the end of the world, the end of man.[11]

After the Holocaust the idea of the Jewish people does not change, but its meaning deepens and its significance extends. The old Hasidic tales become supercharged with more than spiritual significance, as if they had at last become universal stories and the Jew a postmodern Everyman.

Attempts would be made to compromise Wiesel's testimony, to claim his Jewishness makes him one-sided, but the generosity of his witness refutes this criticism and only makes us even more aware of how universal it is to be condemned for one's sectarian commitments. This irony is not lost on Wiesel, who remains an engaged human rights advocate infinitely attuned to the amnesia of history and the deceptive rhetoric of dehumanization. He has spoken out against the Jewish stoning of Palestinians, in favor of giving sanctuary to southeast-Asian refugees, and against Reagan's trip to Bitburg cemetery. Speaking truth to power in the great prophetic tradition, Wiesel lectured Reagan on national television, declaiming "This you must not do!" His plebeianism *is* his Jewish identity, in so far as it serves to connect him to all people who suffer.

He perpetually asserts that to be universal one must first be particular, local, and sectarian; only then are your values existentially authentic, otherwise you are an abstract "humanist" whose real commitment is not to people at all, but to ideas, to systems, to ahistorical man, decontextualized humanity—to air. His quest is to articulate the meaning his Jewish identity holds for our time. It is a meaning that frames history in the form of a question mark; it cannot be reduced to any single idea, thesis, or doctrine. In his novel *Dawn* his main character Elisha remarks, "I have always believed that the mission of the Jews was to be the trembling of History rather than the wind which made it tremble."[12] The same could be said of all indigenous peoples and plebeian communities. And Wiesel's character Kalman the Kabbalist might be speaking for every religious plebeian when he remarks,

> The Jews are God's memory and the heart of mankind. We do not always know this, but the others do, and that is why they treat us with suspicion and cruelty. Memory frightens them. Through us they are linked to the beginning and the end. By eliminating us they hope to gain immortality.[13]

Spirituality in the work of Wiesel is friendship, and evil the reserve that blocks its realization. This reserve has its allies in the ideologies that foster pride and indifference to the sufferings of others, in the slanders that fan fears and militant overreaction. But stories can bridge worlds. And although they cannot work miracles, they can effect some change. They can do some work. They can be useful by uniting individuals in their solitude and inventing, however fictive, a common frame of reference from which to imagine a common future together and so create a sensibility within which our centers may coincide. Without them we are deaf to the reality of the unseen. But with them we have access to our humanity, however smothered it might be by the weight of historical atrocities.

In his work we see several important strands of an evolving postmodern plebeianism:

1. A focus on the importance of tradition, heritage, and the Judaic concept of a people bound to God in endless dialogue and perpetual struggle.

2. A focus upon the Holocaust as a turning point in history demanding a new postmodern ethical vision that goes beyond Camus's absurdist rebellion to a tradition-based affirmation. Wiesel speaks as a Jew and as a survivor, and it is his partisanship that, paradoxically, makes him a universal figure. For given his sense of the Jews' role in history as Other, as refuser, as exception, as problem, as representative of any and all persecuted groups, Wiesel draws universal lessons from a very particular history. He sees his people bound to a destiny as theoretically self-conscious outsiders. This places upon them, especially the Holocaust survivors, a unique historical role as witnesses to truths about life unavailable to the secure, the happy, or the reconciled. Through their eyes tradition has a different meaning, and faith a whole new agenda of responsibilities. Among these are "Never forget" and "Never betray."

3. An exploration of narrative and story as a way beyond materialist history to express the unfolding of the spirit.

4. An examination of "holy madness" as the necessary risk we all must take to survive as Jews, and hence as human beings, in a world where Eichmann is "sane."

5. A focus upon the problems of assimilation as they are writ large in the Jewish experience. The "Jewish Problem" was, and always will be, the problem of a people's resistance to assimilation—their refusal to be absorbed, explained, wiped out, or otherwise co-opted.

6. A renewal of the prophetic role of the messenger: to give hope to the hopeless and pause to the proud.

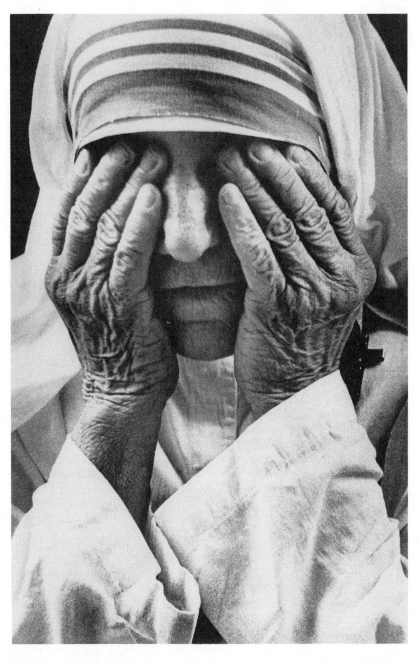

CHAPTER FIVE

Mother Teresa: The Plebeian Pastoral

> When you place your hope in the Lord and sink
> your roots into the concrete power of the poor in
> history, you are not living on nostalgia. You are
> living in a present moment, whose only direction is
> forward.
>
> —GUSTAVO GUTIERREZ[1]

Goodness, like beauty, leaves us mute, unable to speak. And when we finally do produce halting words to express exactly what goodness invokes in us, they always seem weak and inappropriate. So we look to skilled writers and poets to capture for us the words over which saints bound on their way to God.

Many books have been written about Mother Teresa over the years, each attempting to interpret her life or describe her mission. Yet although it sounds odd, most of these biographies, essays, interviews and memoirs end up being unintentionally comic. The clash between Mother Teresa's wordless deeds of love and the rhetorical needs of each genre almost always results in a parody of the authorial voice.

For example, one journalist attempted to uncover the historical origins of Mother Teresa's social mission by interviewing her colleagues from her days teaching at the Loreto High School in Calcutta. To the writer's surprise, many could hardly remember her, and those who did remarked only about her ordinariness. For a Christian servant this lack of recognition may be high praise, but for the uninitiated it strikes one as weak material for a story.

Mother Teresa's interviews and speeches are just as disappointing. She speaks too simply, uses the traditional language of the church, and often replies to sophisticated questions with platitudes and clichés that normally would be dismissed as trite.

Anyone who attempts to interpret Mother Teresa confronts the fact that today's common secular idiom simply lacks the requisite symbolism and moral sensitivity necessary to express adequately the meaning of Christian service. Thus those wanting to write biographies of modern religious thinkers and activists face a difficult challenge: how can simple religious faith be explained to complex secular minds—minds that cannot take seriously the idea of the incarnation of God and so have great difficulty comprehending the character, thought, and actions of one who does.

One of Mother Teresa's most articulate commentators, Malcolm Muggeridge, has said that Christianity must "be grasped through the imagination rather than understood through the mind."[2] When he writes about Mother Teresa, he doesn't use her as an occasion to proselytize or theorize. Rather he tries to get the reader to imagine what the world looks like as seen through her eyes. This is something even he has a difficult time imagining, so he sets this conflict as the central theme of his portrait: How can acutely self-conscious moderns learn to see through the eyes of faith? The result is a profound and moving portrait, not only of Mother Teresa but also of Muggeridge and our own contemporary spiritual landscape. It addresses the world as-it-is about truths it has lost or cannot yet imagine. It invents a new genre: the plebeian pastoral.

It is easy to understand Muggeridge's personal fascination with Mother Teresa; she is, after all, what he is not—an uncomplicated soul. Yet strangely it his status as a complicated modern man that most qualifies him to tell her story. Such status puts him inside a whole set of difficulties that Mother Teresa on her own would never address because they do not strike her as exceptionally problematic. For example, he asked her in an interview for the BBC, "Our fellow men, or many of them, perhaps including myself, have lost their way. You have found the way. How do you help them find the way?" She answered simply, "By getting them in touch with people, for in the people they will find God." But Muggeridge realizes, in a way that the saintly Mother Teresa cannot, the contempt with which most contemporary Western souls hold one another, and so it sounds absurd to suggest to a retail salesman, fast-food worker, junior high vice-principal, or a business tycoon that the people he or she meets every day are the stuff of salvation. So he pressed her a bit: "You mean that the road to faith and the road to God is via our fellow human beings?" To which she replied, "Because we cannot see Christ, we cannot express our love to him; but our neighbours we can always see, and we can do to them what if we saw him we would like to do to Christ . . . in the slums, in the broken body, in the children, we see Christ and we touch him."[3]

Here is a perfectly intelligible, if not eloquent, expression of the principles animating Christian service—but it took a jaded Muggeridge renewed by faith to get Mother Teresa to say it, not just live it. And this is one of the key tasks of Muggeridge's essays: to press upon men and women of faith the spiritual confusions encountered by those less graced in order to extract truths capable of penetrating contemporary defenses and witnessing to otherwise deaf ears. As a result he has invented a new genre of sorts—a kind of postmodern plebeian pastoral where the limitations of the modern are exposed by its incapacity to comprehend an obvious good.

Admittedly Mother Teresa's answer to Muggeridge's question does not address all of the doubts of a modern skeptic. There is no real argument or theology here, and so as a witness for the reality of God it might still only make sense to Christian initiates. Perhaps, Muggeridge should have pressed her even farther and asked "Why touch Christ?" Where does one draw the line in one's exposition of the basic tenets of faith? It is this vital limit that defines the plebeian pastoralist, and I suspect most of today's religious commentators miss the mark, either drawing the line too soon by begging the questions of most skeptics— expressing, in effect, a premodern sensibility—or drawing it too late, only to summarize profound religious experiences in the modern idiom of complex theoretical language that serves to both complicate and oversimplify the deep existential revelations of faith. Muggeridge, when he is successful, manages to resist both premodern platitudes and the watered-down intellectualizations of modernism. By focusing upon the character of Mother Teresa, he keeps a neat balance between an exposition of faith and a respect for the profundity of the Christian mystery. His goal is not to refute objections to Christianity, which are legion, or even to explain it in modern philosophical terms as a legitimate intellectual system. Rather he tries to help us to see the world through the eyes of an exemplary Christian and by so doing grasp its truth via the power of our imaginations.

To do this he sets up a contrast between his commonplace perceptions of the world and Mother Teresa's. Early in his book *Something Beautiful for God*, Muggeridge mentions his brief stay in Calcutta in the nineteen-thirties. At that time he was disgusted by the slums and griped about the wretched social conditions. He remembers asking in disgust and self-righteousness "Why don't the authorities do something?" He quickly left. Mother Teresa, by contrast, saw the same squalor but moved in and stayed—armed, as he puts it, only with "this Christian love shining about her." Muggeridge remarks, "As for my expatiations on Bengal's wretched social conditions—I regret to say that I doubt whether in any divine accounting, they will equal one single quizzical half-smile bestowed by Mother Teresa on a street urchin who happened to catch her eye."[4]

The remark hits home, for we see ourselves and our own glib moral posturing in Muggeridge's confession. Without such commentary Mother Teresa's life would appear merely mythic and lose some of its capacity to challenge us. We can dismiss sainthood as a goal too lofty for ourselves, but we cannot dismiss the way such contrasts throw light on our own moral smugness. Through Muggeridge's self-revelation we see ourselves in relationship to what she has accomplished; moverover, the notion of a divine accounting is used here as both a literary trope and a religious idea. His remark falls both inside and outside a Christian worldview and thereby bridges both the religious and the secular worlds. The "doubt" he expresses is reserved, however, for the value of his secular observations. Muggeridge is clearly coming down on the side of Mother Teresa's Christian commitment, but he lands softly, aware of his own culpability and capacity for sin.

During the previously mentioned BBC interview, Muggeridge, playing the part of a modern social theorist, asked Mother Teresa if there weren't already too many people in India, and if it was worth salvaging a few abandoned children who might otherwise eventually die anyway. The question, Muggeridge reports, was so contrary to her way of viewing the world that she had difficulty grasping it.[5] From a modern point of view such incomprehension registers an incapacity to think beyond one's own values, an inability to grasp ideas impersonally. But from Muggeridge's perspective, confusion in the face of madness is no vice. The confusion is really on our side, and it is to our discredit that we can understand such amoral reasoning so well. For Mother Teresa, all life is sacred, and it is as simple as that. Social theories that contradict this premise are mad.

Muggeridge reflects:

> "What, I wonder, will posterity—assuming that they are at all interested in us and our doings—make of a generation of men, who, having developed technological skills capable of producing virtually unlimited quantities of whatever they might need or desire, . . . were possessed by a panic fear that soon there would not be enough food for them to eat or room for them to live? It will seem, surely, one of the most derisory, ignominious and despicable attitudes to be entertained in the whole of human history."[6]

To an ambitious, self-seeking people constantly fed on the boosterism of our age, this is indeed harsh judgment.

In the stories Muggeridge tells of Mother Teresa's encounters with our world, more dramatic parables emerge. In his introduction to a collection of her prayers and meditations, *A Gift for God*, Muggeridge cites the time she was on a Canadian talk show with a Nobel Prize–

winning biologist who was speculating on the future of DNA break-throughs and the possibility of everlasting biological life. As he spoke, Mother Teresa sat there quietly as if in prayer until the host prodded her to respond to the biologist's mind bending observations. "I believe," she replied, "in love and compassion."[7] The biologist later admitted that the remark had taken him as close as he had ever come to spiritual conversion. Why? Because when Mother Teresa refused to be taken into a universe of discourse alien to her own vision and concerns as a Christian servant, she brought the biologist into hers. This forced him to apply his powerful imagination to seeing himself and his science through her eyes. We can only speculate as to what he saw, but I suspect the resulting juxtaposition of images rivaled Pound's *Cantos* in their power and complexity.

Still, it is Muggeridge's own confessions that bring home the meaning of Mother Teresa's love most powerfully. His admitted conflict with the organized church versus her simple acknowledgment that ecclesiastical squabbles are but things in time and of people, not of God. And the drama of his subsequent acceptance into the Church—primarily through Mother Teresa's influence—speak directly to our modern impatience with the humanity and limitations of our institutions and the necessity for a faith that can see beyond them and find hidden blessings in the pettiness, mediocrity, and even confusion that seems to curse our social lives.

When Muggeridge quotes Mother Teresa's letters, prayers, and talks, he chooses passages that most clearly contradict the modern predilection to judge things by their payoff or practical benefit. For example, he quotes her on holiness:

> "I will be a saint" means I will despoil myself of all that is not God; I will strip my heart of all created things; I will live in poverty and detachment; I will renounce my will, my inclinations, my whims and fancies, and make myself a willing slave to the will of God.[8]

And again, on suffering:

> Without our suffering, our work would just be social work, very good and helpful, but it would not be the work of Jesus Christ, not part of the Redemption. Jesus wanted to help by sharing our life, our loneliness, our agony, our death. . . . We are allowed to do the same; all the desolation of the poor people, not only their material poverty, but their spiritual destitution, must be redeemed, and we must share it, for only by

being one with them can we redeem them, that is, by bringing
God into their lives and bringing them to God."[9]

Such quotations make it very clear why the press mythologizes and
thereby distorts Mother Teresa's significance. To take her seriously as a
manifestation of the possible—not as the saintly exception that proves
the rule of self-interest—would require us to review our most fundamental aims and values. Muggeridge's work makes it clear that she is
just a simple Christian woman with common sense and uncommon
faith; we are the geniuses of amorality.

In our often-mad dash for wealth and self-improvement we sometimes forget that it is possible to be too rich, to have too many choices
and too many resources; they can crowd out the essential and obscure
that higher calling that alone can provide inner sustenance. Robert Bly
speaks of the overwhelming spiritual wealth of the modern individual
who has copies of the Tibetian Book of the Dead, the Bible, and Jung's
essays all on his desk. How can such a one know the spiritual dryness
required for renewal and authentic repentance?[10] We may be simply
too wealthy and too well-informed to confront ourselves. There are far
too many books to read, projects to accomplish, meditation techniques
to master, for us to embrace the wisdom found only on the far side of
grief, poverty, absence, and pain. And yet we must move through this
if we are to escape the barrenness of one-dimensional lives. Scared of
our Jungian shadows, we pursue the *idea* of holiness, a simulacrum of
grace, instead of responding to the moral imperatives, responsibilities,
and strengths or our own higher natures. Thomas Merton describes
the poverty of the new affluence this way:

> When man and his money and machines move out into the
> desert, and dwell there, not fighting the devil as Christ did,
> but believing in his promise of power and wealth, and adoring
> his angelic wisdom, then the desert itself moves everywhere.
> Everywhere is desert. Everywhere is solitude in which man
> must do penance and fight the adversary and purify his heart
> in the grace of God.[11]

It is one thing for Saint John to say "God is love," and quite another
thing when Miss Teen California says it. But even so, there is truth in
each remark—albeit of different kinds. There is no doubt that Muggeridge filters Mother Teresa's witness through his own categories of
understanding, which, one suspects, cannot help but distort its
meaning—a meaning that cannot be explained in anything but theological, maybe even Catholic, terms. And yet Muggeridge has done much

to bring the modern secular mind into sympathy with her on more than simply moral grounds. It is easy to admire her good works, something else again to acknowledge that to her they would mean nothing without Christ and that her greatest work of all is her love—which is, of course, no work at all but a blessing. Muggeridge has clarified this aspect of her witness.

But he has done even more; he has suggested that maybe we cannot fathom her true meaning to our time as a symbol of love because our language and our faith are too weak; that maybe she represents a love our sophisticated frames of reference cannot register; that maybe, after all is said and done, our age is simply so very far off the track that it takes a near saint—with the help of gifted writer—to make our own moral blindness visible to us.

Muggeridge's pastoral strategy is not the only way to accomplish this, but it is unique because it strikes a rare balance between evangelism and academic commentary. I suspect, however, that Muggeridge has just scratched the surface in his invention of a contemporary plebeian pastoral, that there is a complete aesthetic to be found that recoups the traditional spirituality on the other side of both modernism and Marxism: a postmodern plebeianism capable of reading Mother Teresa's life as an action painting.

Perhaps the reason Mother Teresa seems so banal and yet profound when she speaks is that, like an action painting, her mind has become one with her acts. There is no kernel of meaning to be cracked, only a texture of activity to be experienced in its making. She represents a shift from saintly piety to active love, from product to maker, from artwork to performer, from the elaborate delivery systems of the welfare state to small deeds of great love embodied in the concrete touch. We see in her a movement from the disinterested pursuit of the good, true, and the beautiful to the selfless actualization of those same virtues through loving service. Her work in the streets has become the best and only representation of the meaning of her faith.

In this sense, her life does resembles Jerome Klinkowitz's description of postmodern action art:

> The purpose here is not just the production of an art object, but a continuum of events of which the artwork remains as evidence; every piece is in fact a piece of the artist who made it, and its meaning derives from the spectator's appreciation of this totality. [12]

Substitute the word *deed* for *artwork*, and you have a perfect description of Mother Teresa's witness to the West. Its power derives precisely from its antirhetorical "presence." Nothing is hidden, unconscious, derived, but—to quote Harold Rosenberg—each deed is "an *event* out of which a self is formed."[13]

Ever since Alyosha replied to the Grand Inquisitor with a kiss, the exemplary Christian response to intellectual skepticism and moral pain has been love in action. Nowhere can this be seen more clearly than in the person of Mother Teresa, whose very life is a refutation of the common cliché that in our age God is dead. But, of course, we cannot put matters so simply. The modern mind, for some very good reasons, resists the language of faith and positively rejects most traditional religious premises. A new symbolism of deeds is required that could revive our awareness of what we already know—but deepen it and render it part of our behavior. Mother Teresa's life is the stuff of such symbolism, connecting us to truths, spiritual sensibilities, and a sense of sacred obligation *that already exists inside us* but are not yet fully realized.[14]

Mother Teresa's simplicity, humility, and tolerance of other faiths affirms that we must all work within our callings, within our traditions, and within our circumstances to do God's will as it is given us to do. No political ideology need be embraced, no program adopted, only humble service to the reality present to hand. Every frustration or injustice we experience is an opportunity to serve. We need only open up, see, hear, and feel, the address. Mother Teresa has nothing to protect, nothing really to impart; each occasion of service is the recognition of our common brother- and sisterhood under God—the sharing of love that is the joy of the world—and in those occasions, in so far as we respond to them, we do not merely remake ourselves, but we actually discover an authentic unknown: God's will.

But how does one heed God's will? By disengaging from those things that distract us from the divine presence: our idols and addictions. If one is confused as to one's life-calling, one need not hype oneself up with some great ambition or project, one need only remove distractions: listen to others; refrain from anger; pray; make a sacrifice. This seems to be the message Mother Teresa's example imparts to us. Make yourself available to divine influence as it is inscribed in the life experiences all around you.

In *Magister Ludi* also known as *The Glass Bead Game*, Herman Hesse has a student ask his master "Should we pay attention to dreams, master?" To which the master replies, "Yes, pay attention to your dreams." The student then asks, "Can we interpret them?" To which the master replies, "We can interpret everything."[15] Including suffering, including the poor. Mother Teresa remarks:

Today we have no time even to look at each other, to talk
to each other, and still less to be what our children expect from
us, what the husband expects from the wife, what the wife
expects from the husband. And so less and less we are in touch
with each other. The world is lost for want of sweetness and
kindness. People are starving for love because everybody is in
such a great rush.[16]

Mother Teresa's answers to plebeian insufficiency are the ancient
medicines of poverty, chastity, charity, and obedience. What is new
here is their application as a self-consciously counter-modern way of
life. To willingly embrace poverty in all its contemporary manifesta-
tions is to place one's political allegiance with those excluded, either by
choice or by circumstance, from the comforts and false consciousness of
the system at large.

To embrace solidarity with the poor is a revolutionary act of the
most extreme kind, but it is not an act of anarchism nor is it even an act
of political rebellion. It is more simply, and more devastatingly, an act
of refusal—a refusal to live within the economic redefinition and reduction of the ancient mythos—a refusal to acquiesce to the pressures
of secular time and the desacralizing of experience—it is a refusal to
see persons as instrumentalities or commodities.

After a trip to her home for the dying in Calcutta, where he served
as a volunteer, the former Governor of California, Jerry Brown remarked how Mother Teresa's work challenges our entire way of life.
"She lives as if it were God himself lying there in the streets, what does
that mean for how we live each day?"[17] Paraphrasing Gandhi he notes
that we have enough for everyone's need, all we have to do is change
our greed. "But how?" he asks.

Returning to America on the day of the Iowa caucuses
(1988) was odd. I watched a bit of television, and it didn't seem
altogether real: a few babies, some old people, a Veterans of
Foreign Wars hat, slogans. There was a segment about Senator
Paul Simon's inability to talk in short sound bytes and the
impact this would have in a media state. As I watched I wondered: How could I ever take the spirit of Mother Teresa and
apply it to the ordinary world of business and politics? Is there
any connection at all? I think there is. Mother Teresa said over
and over again: "You cannot give what you do not have." And
what she meant was that one's own character has to be good.

You have to have a clean heart if you want to change anything in the world. [18]

A politician, Brown interpreted Mother Teresa's message as a call to virtue in public life. The remark, however true, still falls flat because it has been said before by Richard Nixon and by Dan Quayle. What is needed is some greater recognition of the insufficiency of the public idiom and of our existing political processes. To articulate the meaning of Mother Teresa to our time is to question the spiritual content of everything we say and do.

If none of us can give to the public what we do not have, then there is preliminary work to be done on ourselves—grief to be accepted, creative suffering to be mastered, indulgences and ambitions to be given up, and service to be rendered. The plebeian penchant for the concrete and the particular is not merely a good idea—its not an idea at all—its a redefinition of where reality resides and, so, where it must be confronted. It is unlikely that Brown will be able to formulate any new campaign slogans from his experience in Calcutta; but by internalizing its values he may read the political landscape in a new way—a way that might persuade him not to run for office or a way that might persuade him, if he does, to do so in a new spirit.

When one deals with the poor, the actual poor, as the Sisters of Charity do, one discovers that their needs are as much spiritual as they are material. That is to say, the poor want love as much as they want shelter; they need to be somebody *to somebody* not just receive care from anybody. Mother Teresa tells two poignant "pastoral" stories of her own in this regard.

> Once I picked up a woman from a dustbin and I knew she was dying. I took her out and took her to the convent. She kept on repeating the same words: "My son did this to me." Not once did she utter the words, "I'm hungry," "I'm dying," "I'm suffering." She just kept on repeating: "My son did this to me." It took me a long time to help her say, "I forgive my son," before she died. . . .
>
> Once I picked up a child and took him to our children's home, gave him a bath, clean clothes, everything, but after a day the child ran away. He was found again by somebody else but again he ran away. Then I said to the Sisters: "Please follow that child. One of you stay with him and see where he goes when he runs away. And the child ran away a third time. There under a tree was the mother. She had put two stones under a small earthenware vessel and was cooking something that she

had picked up from the dustbins. The Sister asked the child: "Why did you run away from the home?" And the child said, "But this is my home because this is where my mother is."[19]

The point here is that a plebeian politics begins, not from any social theory of distributive justice or even from the Enlightenment quest to rationally reorganize society, but from the needs and the experiences of actual people and their desires for personal connection.

A Lysistrata of the secular city, Mother Teresa has organized a strike against indifferent contact between persons. A comic figure of grandiose extremes, her mere existence satirizes all our fevered contemporary ambitions. And her postmodern parables expose our moral ignorance in a way unmatched by the concretized abstractions of conventional politicians or Professors of ethics.

Nor could our modernist literary masters have imagined her. Her image appears nowhere in Beckett, Joyce, or Borges. There are hints of her, perhaps, in Wiesel's Hasidic masters, in Solzhenitsyn's zeks, and in Toni Morrison's and Alice Walker's brave Black women, but this is precisely the hidden countertradition of plebeian postmodernism I am attempting to reveal here. It is ethnic, other, the upside down moral vision of those who cannot, or refuse to, accept the values of modernity without correcting its excesses. They form a stark contrast to Norman Mailer's and Philip Roth's existential supermen living out adventures of self-creation inside the urban jungle—surfing the semiotic seas of depersonalized signification in a kind of ecstasy of oblivion. Instead they articulate the revolutionary potential of lost humanism as it lives on in the exiled inner life of the masses.

Within the context of Mother Teresa's work, charity and obedience take on unimagined new meanings, far transcending their reductive dismissal by those who saw them as alienating mystifications. Hers is not the old obligatory charity and pseudo-obedience of conventional bourgeois morality which the modernists were right to reject as a fraud and an evasion. It is rather the challenge not to forget the excluded or the marginalized. It is a public manifestation of the psychoanalytic reclamation of the repressed. It is the classical search for wholeness freed from its exclusionary blinders and linked to the existential demand to act—but to act socially, publicly, for others. If her ethic sometimes sounds reactionary to contemporary ears that is because her language is the ancient, mythic jargon of the Catholic church—an image repertoire with a complex and often compromised history. But Mother Teresa refuses to sever the roots of her own sectarian background, preferring like Gandhi, Solzhenitsyn, King, Walesa and Wiesel to spiritualize and universalize its meaning from within. The problem is not the sectarian imagery; but its parochial and self-interested applications.

But upon what vehicle does one transform the meaning of words except through words themselves? Mother Teresa's answer is through deeds of charity and service. Alyosha's kiss. The plebeian sublime.

A few years ago I saw Mother Teresa on television. It was just after the Beirut bombing by Israel in which so many civilians were killed. Mother Teresa was helping place two wounded little girls into an ambulance when she was accosted by several reporters. One of them asked her if she thought her relief efforts were successful given the fact that there were a hundred other children in another bombed-out hospital that she wasn't getting any aid to. She replied, "Don't you think it is a good thing to help these little ones?" The reporter did not flinch but simply asked his question again: "The other hospital has many wounded children too. Can you call your efforts successful if you leave them unattended?" Mother Teresa ignored his repeated question and, with an obstinacy worthy of an American politician, answered her own: "I think it is a good thing to help these children." She did not say this with scorn, or anger, or even exasperation, but with immovable determination.

And then as her shoulder sank beneath the weight of the stretcher, she gave the reporter a glance that asked, "Why don't you help me lift these children into the ambulance; that is something you can do." It was one of those rare moments, like Alyosha's kiss, when the confusions of the world were defeated, if only for a moment, by a practical act of love. Mother Teresa's love not only for the children but for the reporter in his own moral pain. And I like to think that somewhere in that reporter's soul a hope was sparked, if only for a second, that there was something he could do.

CHAPTER SIX

Martin Luther King: The Plebeian Sublime

> The new world must be built by resolute men who
> "when hope is dead will hope by faith"; who will
> neither seek premature escape from the guilt of
> history, nor yet call the evil, which taints all their
> achievements, good. There is no escape from the
> paradoxical relation of history to the kingdom of
> God. History moves towards the realization of the
> Kingdom but yet the judgement of God is upon
> every new realization.
>
> —REINHOLD NIEBUHR[1]

> The essential claim of the sublime is that man can,
> in feeling and in speech, transcend the human.
> What, if anything, lies beyond the human—God or
> the gods, the daemon or Nature—is matter for
> great disagreement. What, if anything, defines the
> range of the human is scarcely less sure.
>
> —THOMAS WEISKEL, The Romantic Sublime[2]

It is over two decades since Martin Luther King, Jr., was murdered and almost a decade since his birthday was declared a national holiday, and yet America is just beginning to hear what he had to say. His prophetic message is coming to us little by little, piece by piece, as we move away from the racist, politicized misreadings of his life to a fuller appreciation of his heroic stature. By now his dream that we might all be judged by the content of our characters and not by the color of our skin has become an American proverb—if hardly a reality. But certain other lessons he taught are still largely ignored, and in many cases completely misunderstood by the country at large. These are his lessons on nonviolence, his call to a life of character and service, and his reminders of the true meaning of leadership and social responsibility.

My guess is that in time, given the momentum of his fame and historical status, even these lessons will make their ways into the American history books, if not America's conscience. But as of now, he is largely remembered as a civil rights leader and not for what he truly was: an American sage.

But if Martin Luther King, Jr., was a sage, he was a peculiar one—compelled by his times to play the prophet, the martyr, the tragic hero, and eventually the saint, when his genius resided in his voice: in his incredible capacity to link the grand conception to the passionate utterance, to speak the (let us call it) "plebeian sublime."

For the meaning of the sublime, I like Harold Bloom's definition:

> as the mode of literary agon, the struggle on the part of every person to answer the triple question concerning the contending forces of past and present: more? equal to? or less than? Longinus and Shelly also imply that the literary sublime is the reader's sublime, which means that the reader must be able to defer pleasure, yielding up easier satisfactions in favor of a more delayed and difficult reward. That difficulty is an authentic mark of originality, an originality that must seem eccentric until it usurps psychic space and establishes itself as a fresh center.[3]

Few political leaders approach the sublime because few politicians are also visionaries. But only those who are visionary can provide the kind of leadership that can inspire greatness. Lincoln achieved the sublime, as did Churchill and Gandhi—articulating a "delayed and difficult reward" and establishing a "fresh center" to national identity. And although the sublime and plebeian concerns are not usually associated with each other, they merge in the traditions of Old Testament prophecy, African-American oratory, and in the person of Martin Luther King, Jr., who called on his people *as a people* to live out their destiny as the moral educators of humanity.

When he was only twenty-six years old, King told those gathered at the first meeting of the Montgomery bus boycott, "If you will protest courageously, and with dignity and Christian love, when the history books are written in future generations, the historians will have to pause and say, 'There lived a great people—a black people—who injected new meaning into the veins of civilization.' This is our challenge and our overwhelming responsibility."[4]

King believed that an energized and spiritualized Black America in possession of its self-respect and committed to change could heal at the deepest ontological levels, as well as at the most practical and existen-

tial levels, the diseased psyche of racist America and by so doing rock
an empire the same way the early Christians had once rocked Rome. To
do so they would have to find the form, the language, and the will to
mobilize their quest for justice even if the white majority of Americans
simply refused to recognize the problem. He found the form in
Gandhian nonviolence, the language in the Bible, and the will in the
just indignation of Black Americans. But it was his particular gift to
synthesize all three of these ingredients in his voice, a voice that shook
the very foundations of the American conscience.

Taylor Branch, in his epic history of the civil rights movement in
the United States, *Parting the Waters* (1988), tells a story that illustrates King's unique access to the plebeian sublime. In 1957 King was
preparing a speech on voter rights for the Prayer Pilgrimage to Washington. He would be addressing the largest live audience of his career,
and he had filled his speech with the phrase, *Give us the ballot.* One of
his advisors, Bayard Rustin, objected to the phrase as too deferential,
asking King to replace it with *We demand the ballot.* King tried out
various alternatives aloud such as *When we achieve the ballot.* But none
of them sounded right to him, so he kept *Give us the ballot,* to Bayard
Rustin's dismay. Rustin was sure the phrase would get King branded
weak and ineffective. But the phrase worked—there were no criticisms
and no suggestions of weakness. Rustin concluded that he must have
overestimated the role of content in public oratory.[5]

But such an interpretation underestimates both King's nuanced
rhetorical ear and moral complexity. Anyone who hears that speech—
and there are recordings available—hears irony, outrage, even threat
in King's reiteration of "Give us the ballot!" The phrase reverberates
against itself—builds as the speech builds—and never means quite the
same thing twice. It is hardly deferential. And when you join that
phrase with the man—his bearing, the look in his eye—other emo-
tions attend the phrase that are almost too subtle to describe: relief that
truth is finally being told, respect that one of us was brave enough to
speak it, and pity and fear for the man so destined to embody it. Also a
kind of shame that one finds oneself learning for the first time things
one thought one already knew—almost as if whatever King said, however banal the truism, one was hearing it for the very first time.

Such effects could not derive from merely histrionic ability. King
had an instinct for what phrases he could speak with conviction, what
phrases would carry home the truth of his message to the heart of his
listeners through his own personal passion. Such judgment was an
index of how well he knew himself and how well he understood how
who he was qualified and measured what he said.

In a postmodern setting King's themes of the redemptive power of agape, the moral ecology of divine providence, the sacredness of the human personality, and the moral obligation to resist structures of oppression take on a peculiar new prescience. It is as if what once appeared plebeian, indigenous, and localized in a moment of social history is emerging as something larger than anyone had previously imagined. From his struggles against racism and his attempts to go beyond the modern clash between liberalism and neo-orthodoxy in theology, there emerged a profound new understanding of the human will as both a vehicle for change and the most precious of human attributes. This defense of the deep self, forged as it was in struggles to redeem everyday life from the unconscious barbarism of racism in the United States, turned out to be the first and perhaps only public assault upon the new totalitarian impulses unleashed into the world as a result of World War II. Not that racism in the United States was a postwar phenomenon, but its mechanisms, its systematic brutality, stood revealed as part and parcel of the fascist plague that had already desecrated Europe.

Looking back now on what King accomplished, we see more than just a tactician for civil rights; we see a postmodern plebeian philosopher—someone who applied the insights gained from his technical work in theology to public issues. He gave philosophical and theological meaning to the economic and social conflicts confronting the nation, transforming the fight for a more "just" segregation policy on Montgomery buses into a national debate over the meaning of justice in America.

Unlike Malcolm X, King embraced nonviolence as the means for combating the fascist temptation built into any ideological critique of the mechanisms of power. But rather than compare him to Malcolm X, which has been done many times before, it might be a useful approach to follow Taylor Branch's lead and describe King's unique intellectual and political achievements by contrasting him to his counter-parts in the white establishment: John F. Kennedy and Reinhold Niebuhr.[6] This has the advantage of shifting the terms of comparison from who was the better Black leader to the new vision King trying to impart to a resistant, and largely self-satisfied American status quo.

From King's point of view, Black liberation required a new vision of civic virtue born of moral transformation. This view contrasted sharply with Kennedy's political style of deft and daring maneuvering within the parameters of a rather conservative understanding of the mechanisms of power. For King such realpolitik—especially considering the President's own rather weak civil rights record—did not bespeak presidential realism so much as a shortsightedness as to the larger moral dynamics at work within the nation. In his dazzling essay

"Superman Comes to the Supermarket," Norman Mailer described Kennedy as an existential hero whose greatest accomplishment was to re-create himself, to forge an identity as president, to dare to live the American myth that "each one of us was born to be free, to wander, to have adventure and grow on the waves of the violent, the perfumed, the unexpected."[7] From Mailer's perspective, Kennedy was the Nietzschean Superman in the American political supermarket; his heroic stature transcended mere media hype to reflect a too-long-repressed longing of the American psyche for the cool, the daring, the dashing, the wild, the resourceful "brave gun."

But seen from below, from the view of the downtrodden, the poor, the excluded, and the Black, the triumph of this particular incarnation of American frontier mythology—however liberal its rhetoric—lacked a serious appreciation of the prices paid and still being paid by others, upon which these self-created Camelots were built. The theatre of history is not a empty stage for an existential hero living on the edge; it is a drama already in full swing. We enter it with deep obligations that define us more powerfully and completely than we can ever comprehend, moral imperatives that transcend the political machinations of modernist political power brokers. As King could never forget, we are born into a people, an ethnicity, an historical moment, and hence a destiny. For him much more was at stake in our policies than our national mood. Our character and souls were on the line. And so a public man must live with a debt of gratitude to the people from which he emerged as a human being. He cannot simply "make" policy according to his own intellectual lights or those of the best and the brightest around him. Such an approach may be creative, often even brilliant, but it is inevitably thin and historically superficial. He must respond to the deep moral needs of his time.

Kennedy simply failed the test of vision—perhaps no living white American public figure could have met it at that time. But if Kennedy was the modernist American Superman who coupled the glamour of a movie star with the audacity of empire, Martin Luther King represented a far different character type—something as yet unseen and ungrasped—the individual in whom simple moral conviction was linked to a complex intellect capable of penetrating the subterfuges of power and, thus, opening the way to a greater national destiny.

In *The Minimal Self* (1984) Christopher Lasch remarks:

> The distinguishing characteristic of selfhood, however,
> is not rationality but the critical awareness of man's divided
> nature. Selfhood expresses itself in the form of a guilty con-

science, the painful awareness of the gulf between human
aspirations and human limitations.[8]

This tragic self, this Christian self, is the dynamic plebeian self. Its
inward division is a precondition, indeed a given, of one's humanity.
Dialectics, because it subsumes the individual will within the larger
historical Will, can only describe resolved conflicts of the past or emerging conflicts of the future from the still point of an all-knowing theoretical reflection. But in the present, it is helpless, unable to grapple
with fear, hope, grief, or the absurd; unable to see the unconditional
existential options emerging all around it; it can only examine them
after the fact. The deconstructive postmodern analyses of desire do a
better job of describing these options but give up any connections with
the past, so they end up liberating the subject to the play of libidinal
energy across the semiotic surface of the ever new commercial world
system at the cost of any and all inward tension.

King's ethic, however, not only bears in on the choices individuals
make but dares to assess them based upon a specific reading of the past
as it is inscribed on the present—in the physiognomy of its injustices.
In Being's struggle with Becoming, one finds oneself written, as it
were, across the sky of historical change. And with an awareness of this
comes responsibility: the recognition that one's quest for meaning and
dignity can only be realized in an activation of the will against the will-
less-ness, the inhumanity, of the perpetual round. In other words,
against the conditional life and the "boredom of the good mind that
acquiesces to it." Doing God's will is, in this sense, maintaining the
unconditional possibility against the deterministic mindset that is always seeking the single best tactic—or demanding the rigid doctrinal
absolute.

Niebuhr had criticized Gandhi's attempt to introduce religion into
politics, by arguing that nonviolence was itself coercive—that it too
could lead to violence—and that any attempt to collapse these two
realms was impossible and only inflated the politician's inevitable
power plays under false pretenses of morality. In politics love was not
possible; only the negative good of justice was possible, and one had to
use power and coercion to enforce it. Humanity could not be per-
suaded to be selfless—its intelligent selfishness, entrenched as it was
in collectivities, could only be checked by structures of power, and the
Christian realist had to affirm this paradox or risk inflating her or his
partial truth (as a social being) into an absolute, thereby denying the
conditionality of her or his political claims.

At first King accepted this view, and his use of boycotts and mass demonstrations is an acknowledgment of the need for coercion to accompany moral suasion if justice is to be achieved. But King's epiphanies and religious experiences in the movement gave him a glimpse of human possibility that Niebuhr's realism did not explain. King remarks:

> The experiences in Montgomery did more to clarify my thinking in regard to the question of nonviolence than all of the books that I had read. As the days unfolded, I became more and more convinced of the power of nonviolence. Nonviolence became more than a method to which I gave intellectual assent; it became a commitment to a way of life. Many issues I had not cleared up intellectually concerning nonviolence were now resolved within the sphere of practical action.[9]

Buried within this remark are the profound emotional experiences of that first campaign—dealing with the anger, responding to the obfuscations and the pressure tactics, undergoing arrest, becoming a national figure, having his house bombed and his life threatened. Yet King still affirmed nonviolence—beyond Niebuhr's admission of its tactical usefulness within certain limited circumstances—as a way of life, a way to transfigure himself and heal those caught in the tragic conflicts generated by the civil rights struggle.

In a 1965 *Playboy Magazine* interview, King mentioned how the bombing of the 16th Street Baptist Church in Birmingham, in which four little girls were murdered as they sat in their Sunday-school class, made him ask whether, if men are this bestial, the struggle is worth it. Is there any hope? Is there any way out? The interviewer asks, "Do you still feel this way?" King responds:

> No, time has healed the wounds—and buoyed me with the inspiration of another moment which I shall never forget: when I saw with my own eyes over three thousand young Negro boys and girls, totally unarmed, leave Birmingham's 16th Street Baptist Church to march to a prayer meeting— ready to pit nothing but the power of their bodies and souls against Bull Connor's police dogs, clubs and fire hoses. When they refused Connor's bellowed order to turn back, he whirled and shouted to his men to turn on the hoses. It was one of the most fantastic events of the Birmingham story that these Negroes, many of them on their knees, stared, unafraid and

unmoving, at Connor's men with the hose nozzles in their hands. Then slowly the Negroes stood up and advanced, and Connor's men fell back as though hypnotized, as the Negroes marched on past to hold their prayer meeting. I saw there, I felt there, for the first time the pride and the *power* of nonviolence.[10]

Nonviolence goes beyond the tragic awareness of Christian realism to affirm an epiphanic realm in history where God's will exposes itself in new, unimagined, undreamed-of possibilities. It is as if in affirming the paradoxical clash of moral man against immoral society, King dis- covered the God of liberation theology. "I AM WHO I WILL BE."[11] This synthesis of essentialist philosophical theology with dialectics takes place in the street, in practice, in the struggle itself. It is not exactly the triumph of practical reason over theory so much as the recognition that certain limit conditions exposed by the philosophical theology of Niebuhr can sometimes be transcended by communities of faith committed to the practice of nonviolence. Such moments of tran- scendence do not invalidate the Christian sense of paradox between the unconditioned soul and the very conditional realms of history—but they do give rise to hope.

Bill Kellermann points out that another weakness in Niebuhr's views was his sense of audience.[12] It is one thing to argue that one must temper one's utopian longings for the beloved community with a sense of the inevitable self-interestedness of the collectives, when one is tempering the excesses of a fanatical popular movement such as fascism or communism; but to voice such a view in the United States in the fifties, when no popular movement existed to check government excesses or order populist public priorities, did not qualify the spirit of reform so much as explain away its absence. Niebuhr's thought as- sumes a public in tension with its ruling structures—pleading its own agenda, pushing at the seams of the systems that contain it—not an imbalance of power where the conformist masses acquiesce to their own growing political obsolescence in the face of an expanding state hegemony. In such a context the Christian paradox can all too easily become an excuse for duplicity—a reason for rejecting human soli- darity as a utopian mirage and social reform as wishful thinking.

Eventually King would go so far as to turn Niebuhr's philosophy on its head.[13] Niebuhr's doctrine was that private virtue was possible but public virtue was impossible, and yet King's experience in Montgom- ery had taught him quite a different lesson: he had performed a miracle of public virtue, and yet he was more aware than ever of his own personal capacity for sin. Personal evil seemed more intractable than social evil, contradicting the key thesis in Niebuhr's *Moral Man and Immoral Society* (1932).

King's sexual adventurism—testified to by his best friend, the late Ralph Abernathy, in his courageous book *And the Walls Came Tumbling Down* (1989)—may seem to contradict one of the key lessons of Mother Teresa: that moral transformation *precedes* effective social service. But there is an important difference between moral transformation defined as initiation into a life of struggle and moral transformation defined as realized perfection. They are not the same. King's moral vision functions in spite of his personal failures, and in some ways his own analysis of the moral dialectic becomes even more poignant in light of it.

[In a sermon on overcoming sin, King defined two ways to resist temptation. One could employ the tactic of Odysseus and plug the ears of one's crew with wax, tie oneself to the mast, and push on past the sirens. Or one could employ the method of Orpheus and compose a song more beautiful than anything the sirens had to offer.\King recommends the way of Orpheus. And if he himself failed to overcome temptation, we can still admire the beautiful vision he affirmed in his speeches, in his ideas, and in his public life.

Mother Teresa's virtues have often been misrepresented by the press's portraying her as the exception that proves the rule of self-interest, whereas King's influence is undermined by an attack upon his less-than-perfect private life. These are two sides of the same reactionary strategy of self-justification:\If one is moral, then one is not normal and, therefore, not a model; if one is fallible, then one is normal, and therefore not a model either.\ In either case the sublime is rejected as an unreal aspiration for ordinary souls, and its advocates dismissed as surreal saints or pious frauds.

But plebeian postmodernists eschew perfectionist ideals and utopian schemes to affirm the struggle of those born again into the quest for greatness. King's odd destiny, not unlike Paul's, was to have grasped a world-shattering vision before his life could completely embody it. This is no refutation of the vision; on the contrary, it is testimony to the reach of his political and moral imagination.

This vision now seems similar to that of liberation theology in that King sees God's will unfolding before him—not as an atemporal truth, eternal, but as an omnitemporal truth becoming what it will be in the very moment that it is. King's personalism and respect for dialectics lead him to sense the limitations of any essentialist theological anthropology—even one so wise as Niebuhr's—that defines humanity before all the evidence of history is in. Yet, unlike the liberation theologians, King is not a total dialectician; he adheres to a philosophical theology that holds fast to a personal God of history and the paradox of the cross. His dialectics is qualified by a sense of the tragic and the otherwordly, and synthesized with personalism and nonviolence.

His teacher at Boston University Edgar S. Brightman espoused an

> epistemological dualism of "the shining present" and "the illuminating absent." Immediate experience is the inescapable starting point, but experience always refers beyond itself (self-transcendence). The possibility of reference is found in the activity of the mind in knowing; the adequacy of the reference is determined by the criterion of coherence. Maximum coherence in interpreting experience is maximum truth. In his emphasis on the tentativeness and testing of hypotheses, Brightman was empirical; in his emphasis upon system and inclusive order, he was rationalistic.[14]

King sees this same dualism operating in nonviolence—only nonviolence articulates an ethic of engagement with the dilemmas of one's age. In Gandhian nonviolence King had discovered a way to overcome the plebeian vices without destroying their virtues—a way that linked the subtle Christian realism of Reinhold Niebuhr with the existential heroism of Rosa Parks.[15]

King's status as a postmodern can be seen in how his synthesis transforms certain key modernist preoccupations. The search for a method gets transformed into a dialectical, nonviolent way of life. Alienation is not simply an existential given but evidence of frustrated communication, the product of segregation among races, among cultures, and among aspects of the self. Love is not a private state but a form of communication. It cannot exist in isolation from human community. Individualism finds its highest expression in sociability and service.

Moreover, King's religious assumptions free him from the modernist will to a system, since the foundation of all his thought is not an idea but a person and a set of images entering into an uncertain, unfolding future. The modern interest in surfaces and forms, for King, is evidence of an incomplete philosophical analysis, the ahistorical bent of a mind cut off from struggle and therefore from human solidarity. In linking the civil rights movement with the peace movement, King in his prime intuited the universal significance of his perspective as the harbinger of a new ethic no longer content to subordinate conscience to the increasingly powerful social structures of commerce and government.

One can only imagine his response to certain postmodern themes in theology and politics, such as the new antifoundationalism in metaphysics. One suspects personalism may sidestep this issue, since its sense of reality as personhood is operational and so requires no foundation per se. As to the relativity of much contemporary ethics, King would no doubt have offered a dialectical yes-and-no. Yes, conditional situations define the good in limited ways. No, there are absolutes even given the conditionality of history. Persons are always ends, never merely means.

For the modern culture to function, people must be pried away from their traditions. King's linkage of the civil rights movement to the peace movement was a bold frontal assault upon this contemporary trend. The enemy was now no longer ignorant, backward, white bigots, but the emerging global economic system that capitalism had become, with all its corollary reactions to the emerging worldwide pressure for freedom and personhood. In place of the ceaseless self-transformations of style characteristic of the industrialized nations, King advocated a well-formed interior life coupled with a Gandhian activism to force the social structures into acknowledging the continuities of history and the worth of the individual person. His vision demanded not only an engaged life but a militant one. His basic assumptions were that the collective would not be just unless compelled to be so, nor could it be humane unless purged from within by spiritually transformed individuals.

But how does one accomplish this kind of reform? King offered many practical solutions, but they can be boiled down to essentially three strategies: 1) Loving one's enemies, 2) overcoming one's fears, and 3) combating evil through faith and nonviolent noncooperation. Let's look at these one by one.

One of the postmodern insights in King's understanding of nonviolence is his view that not only does a transforming vision of society come from below, but those on the bottom are the only ones with the power to heal the whole—not through armed rebellion or a dictatorship of the proletariat, but through their power to forgive. And those in power must find the contrition of heart to accept their forgiveness. In order to forgive, the oppressed must recognize the injustice of their situation and their inherent superiority to it. And those in power, in order to be contrite, must recognize their collusion with sin and do penance. By refusing to ignore injustice but also refusing to let it block further relationship, the wronged minority posits a more inclusive vision of human solidarity than those "profiting" from inequality could dare imagine. And by seeking out a relationship they have long denied, the powerful find moral direction—perhaps for the very first time. This superiority of vision is not moral one-upmanship, but rather a clarity of purpose that links nonviolent revolutionaries to a force greater than themselves, breaking the shackles of any residual sense of inferiority and thus making possible a more powerful form of self-affirmation than one's enemy could ever achieve. King remarked:

> I think the greatest victory of this period was . . . something internal. The real victory was what this period did to the psyche of the black man. The greatness of this period was that we armed ourselves with dignity and self-respect. The greatness of this period was that we straightened our backs up. And a man can't ride your back unless it's bent.[16]

Another key nonviolent concept is King's idea that the evil the enemy may do never expresses all that he or she is. This philosophical anthropology of hope is a wager not so much on the goodness of humanity, but on its infinite complexity. It asserts that in the depths and turmoil of the inner life—that realm of the will that is by definition divided against itself—reside mysteries and potentialities beyond our own or even our enemies' own self-descriptions. New regions within the enemy can be reclaimed, and they can become battlegrounds for the good. Grief, love, devotion, the language of praise, hope, and contrition can open new spaces in the heart, zones of reform in the other, new avenues of reconciliation. Such is the expansive geography of the spiritual life, and the nonviolent front encompasses the entire terrain.

In seeking to redeem the enemy, not defeat him, King also moves beyond the epic conceits of the warrior mythologies to a critique of the triumphant self-over-others mythology. Echoing Simone Weil's protofeminist analysis of the *Illiad*, he asserts that only those who know the glory of violent battle and are not impressed by it can truly bring about a new dispensation on the other side of heroic individualism. This requires a more concrete sense of the unity of being than traditional Western heroics allows, or the ascending new barbarisms deconstruct. It demands a confrontation with the shadow selves living in all our paranoid projections and fearful denials.

Adam Michnik—a Polish dissident Solidarity member who after spending many years in government prisons is now a member of the Polish congress—wrote an essay exploring many of these same dynamics, entitled "Why You Are Not Signing. . . A Letter from Bialoeka Internment Camp 1982." In that piece he argued that there were at least three good arguments for not signing the communist party's loyalty declarations even though refusal could mean ending up in prison or out of work. The first argument is that it just isn't worth it. Life

outside a prison in a concentra   g than
living with a free conscience ir   aterial
inducements are so trivial the   nent is
from common sense. Once oi   eapon.
Capitulation is self-betrayal on a practical, indeed ever., , level.
One can't enter into agreements with the police on their terms and
expect anything good to come of it. The third argument is from memory. History shows that in the long run, over time, the servile are
forgotten, the true patriots remembered. In the history of his people a
loyalty oath signed in prison has always been a disgrace, loyalty to
oneself and the national tradition always a virtue. He remarks:

> Solidarity has never had a vision of the ideal society. It
> wants to live and let live. Its ideals are closer to the American
> Revolution than to the French. . .it is unlike the thinking of
> those who strive to attain doctrinal goals. The ethics of Soli-
> darity, with its consistent rejection of the use of force, has a lot
> in common with the idea of nonviolence as espoused by
> Gandhi and Martin Luther King, Jr.[17]

What Solidarity has in common with King's approach is this sense
of combating totalitarian structures of oppression by a studied refusal
to become totalitarian oneself—to reject rigid doctrinal views, to keep
alive the unconditional possibility buried beneath the enemy's bullying
strategies or Machiavellian tactics.

In this sense the quest for justice is not a utopian dream or an
idealism. On the contrary, idealistic visions are the seeds of totalitarian
oppressions. Nonviolent noncooperation with evil is the practical act of
affirming one's dignity and the common ground of history against the
gun-toting Idealists attempting to keep secure their fantasies of power.

But as clear as this might seem, fear often clouds our minds and
obscures our best intentions. When you are the victim of injustice or
the object of hatred, it is not always so easy to know that it is not worth
it to betray oneself, or to remember the lessons of the past, or even to
cling to common sense. King in one of his sermons offers antidotes to
fear that affirm the deep self and redefine the traditional Christian
verities in terms of existential struggle.

First he tells us one must face one's fears and sort out the real from
the imaginary. Then, once the real dangers are recognized, they must
be met with courage—which King defines in Tillich's terms as self-
affirmation *in spite of* "that which tends to hinder the self from affirming itself."[18] Courage, in this sense, is the power of the mind over
fear—a determination not to let obstacles or life's ambiguities block

our affirmation of life. Courage is the realization that nothing is so much to be feared as fear itself.

Such self-affirmation *in spite of* the conditional difficulties of life, can do much to lift us above our circumstances and define our character—giving substance to our lives and dignity to our aspirations, and setting us down the path of righteousness. King remarked:

> Thucydides, that eminent student of the human saga, touched upon a lasting truth in his funeral speech for Pericles when he said, "The secret of happiness is freedom, and the secret of freedom, courage."[19]

But Christian love, agape, is the key to *enduring* the struggle, allowing us to confront evil without flinching and allowing us to demonstrate "an infinite capacity to take it."[20] Love casts out the enemy's fear and by so doing begins to tame his hatred. By loving our adversary, we wish the best for them—and that is conversion of the enemy into our ally.

Robert Coles, the child psychiatrist, tells the story of when he was writing psychological appraisals of the children integrating the elementary schools in the South during the early sixties. Everyday Ruby Bridges, age six, had to walk to school through a line formed by National Guardsmen surrounded by angry whites shouting out threats and racist epithets, and yet none of it ever seemed to bother her. When he asked her what she thought of all those angry people who shouted at her, she replied that she felt sorry for them, and that every night she and her mother prayed that they would find Jesus.[21] This is the kind of transforming love King wished to build his movement upon.

But such love does not come without faith, and this is the next point of King's "ladder" sermon. "Let us face the fear that the atomic bomb has aroused with the faith that we can never travel beyond the arms of the divine."[22] One need not depend upon one's own personal power to love; there are, as it were, absolutes, laws, forces in the universe infinitely more potent than our tiny wills, and faith is the mechanism through which we insert ourselves within their power and grace.

King tells the story of a troubled time and of a sermon he gave that lacked his usual power and conviction. Mother Pollard, a member of his congregation, came up to him afterward and asked him what was wrong, and he pretended that nothing was the matter.

> "Now you can't fool me," she said. "I knows something is wrong. Is it that we ain't doing things to please you? Or is it

that the white folks is bothering you?" Before I could respond, she looked directly in my eyes and said, "I don told you we is with you all the way." Then her face became radiant and she said in words of quiet certainty, "But even if we ain't with you, God's gonna take care of you." As she spoke these consoling words, everything in me quivered and quickened with the pulsing tremor of raw energy."[23]

James Cone tells of a time when King received a particularly nasty death threat over the phone. King received on the average forty death threats per day.[24] But this one caused him to lose his courage, and he sought a way to withdraw from the movement. Cone reports:

> He went to the kitchen and prayed: "Lord, I'm down here trying to do what's right. I think I'm right. I think the cause we represent is right. But, Lord, I must confess that I'm weak now; I'm faltering, I'm losing my courage; and I can't let the people see me like this because if they see me weak and losing courage, they will begin to get weak." At that moment Martin said he heard an inner voice saying to him: "Martin Luther, stand up for righteousness. Stand up for justice. Stand up for truth. And lo, I will be with you until the end of the world."[25]

There may be little new here theologically, but what is always new in every act of faith is its particular application. Newness in itself is a modernist value—constructive postmoderns and plebeians seek renewal, and that comes from existential attention to how the traditional absolutes play against the ever-unique present. In the Mother Pollards of this world we see a long-suffering devotion to the best in themselves that embodies levels of conviction only obtainable through years of life experience.

So enamoured are we of the psuedosophistication of complication that we often miss the profoundity in simple virtue. This is especially true in matters of religion and politics, where concrete acts of courage and self-sacrifice often get obscured in the rhetorics of political justification, policymaking, and procedural recommendations. Mother Teresa's simple acts of love, for example, are almost unintelligible to those in the modern media who must explain her "theories" to a modern audience almost totally abstracted from direct experience—born, as it were, into an entirely commercially mediated environment, culturally marked from the first pair of disposable diapers to the last television game-show beamed into its hospital room.

The point here is that in describing these concrete antidotes to fear, King is both urging resistance to current oppression and describing a perennial ethic—updating the values of courage, love and faith by showing how they might operate in our own everyday lives. He is not trying to describe a phenomenology of the will so much as to correct the plebeian vice of self-interest by linking it to the greater historical destiny of his people as moral educators. He is tapping the wellsprings of traditional virtues by making them intelligible again in a world turned upside down. He tries to point out that the difficulty, as Socrates puts it in the *Apology*, is not to avoid death but to avoid unrighteousness. Or as King himself put it, "Death is not the ultimate evil, the ultimate evil is to be outside God's love."[26]

King's final imperative—to resist the structures of evil—involves King directly in all the issues raised by contemporary liberation theology. And although his thought on these matters was more in dialogue with Niebuhr's Christian "realism" and Rauschenbusch's social gospel than with thinkers like Boff or Gutierrez, his insights still possess striking contemporary relevance.

In his sermon "The Answer to a Perplexing Problem," King addressed the question, How can evil be cast out of our collective and individual lives? He rejects waiting on God, and he rejects taking history into our own hands. Instead he articulates a third option:

> Both man and God, made one in a marvelous unity of purpose through an overflowing love as the free gift of himself on the part of God and by perfect obedience and receptivity on the part of man, can transform the old into the new and drive out the deadly cancer of sin.[27]

To change the world we must become receptacles of God's love, mutual respect, understanding, and good will. We must have not merely the faith of the mind, but the faith of the heart that surrenders the whole person to the divine inflow. This is a departure from Niebuhr's dualism, which admits a metanoia of the soul but not of the community, in that it links personal salvation directly to social responsibility, and it is a departure from progressive liberalism because it sets divine limits to change and to one's own capacity to effect change. Victory is not the goal—doing God's will is.

One sees here all the great themes of liberation theology—the primacy of persons over structures, a preference for the poor, a rejection of both individualism and collectivism for the participatory beloved community, and the moral obligation to resist collective evil.

The shattered dream of a nonviolent transformation of the American character and the subsequent disillusions of Watergate, Contragate, and the Reagan "revolution" would have represented to King not so much defeat as a dialectical movement that must be responded to by pressure from the people to defend themselves against the growing marginality of their personhood. Again King found his inspiration in the example of the early Church and in the figure of the Apostle Paul. Rejecting bitterness, resignation, and withdrawal, King advises taking up the burden of one's disappointments and by so doing transforming them into challenges. "Our willing acceptance of unwanted and unfortunate circumstances even as we still cling to radiant hope, our acceptance of finite disappointment even as we adhere to infinite hope. This is not the grim, bitter acceptance of the fatalist, but the achievement found in Jeremiah's words, 'This is a grief, and I must bear it.'"[28]

The postmodern cultural condition has been described as a field of shattered dreams, a world whose hope is less than zero. Indifference and complacency abound, fueled by a false sense of affluence and an ideology of privilege. Intellectually-half-dead plebeians celebrate the democracy of culture through their own self-defeating pursuits of wealth and self-sufficiency. The old Jeffersonian dream of economically independent, hence free, farmers has degenerated into a search for financial independence via multimarketing schemes, real-estate clubs, and lotto tickets. Gone are the politics of the sublime. As our collective lives wither, our imaginations disappear, and the mass media becomes ever more spectacular and specious. The middle class purchases self-help books in an effort to teach themselves how to see their lives as commodities so as to overcome any residual personhood that might be holding them back from complete success. Gone is our humanity and, as Allan Bloom has argued, gone are our humanities. King stands as the dreamer, the challenging counterexample to the new "stupidity" masking itself in feigned, hedonistic delight and to the fanatical, antidialectical schemes of those who would save us from ourselves at the cost of our creative intelligence and personal authenticity: the cultists, the Oliver Norths, the survivalists—the enemies of our collective life. King synthesized dialectics as creative history with both personalism (defined as the dignity of the individual) and faith (defined as the hope that sustains the beloved community.)

Reactionary rhetoric—the antisublime—tends to regularize, trivialize, minimize, legalize, and neutralize moral issues. It is pharisaic—thriving on legalistic and technical distractions. The plebeian sublime thrives on the larger moral and spiritual dimensions of things. It aggrandizes, synthesizes, makes links across the ages and across classes to join the shining present with the illuminating absent. Its enemy is the superficial, the easy, the course of least resistance—the merely workable. King articulated the plebeian sublime at that first mass meeting for the bus boycott in Montgomery when he dared to link that small dispute within segregation law to the injustices experienced by Isaiah and the timeless struggle for human dignity itself.

> We are not wrong in what we are doing. If we are wrong—
> the Supreme Court of this nation is wrong. If we are wrong—
> God almighty is wrong! If we are wrong—Jesus of Nazareth
> was merely a utopian dreamer and never came down to earth!
> If we are wrong—justice is a lie. And we are determined here
> in Montgomery—to work and fight until justice runs down
> like water, and righteousness a mighty stream![29]

There are admittedly limits to the plebeian sublime in terms of practical politics. The SNCC organizer Bob Moses warned as early as 1963 that unless the civil rights movement keyed upon the issues of universal suffrage for dispossessed Blacks, it ran the risk of making lasting gains only for the Black bourgeoisie. King knew this, fought this, and to some extent would no doubt be slightly embarrassed by his current status as the secular saint of bourgeois civil rights reforms. His message was more than this—his voice more profound and more pained than the simple celebration of spiritual equality his words are often reduced to. Martin Luther King was, in the words of one of his parishioners, "a God-troubled man," distressed by America's incapacity to grasp the beauty of its own Black population. And so he tried to educate us through his words, his deeds, his voice, and his life— through the postmodern curriculum of nonviolent noncooperation with evil—to the spiritual beauty of the great Black plebeian sublime. His accomplishment was to achieve his heritage, to realize its presence within himself, his people, and his circumstances. The King phenomenon, if we can call it that, was a miracle of responsibility. Perhaps it is still too early to measure his success because it is still being realized.

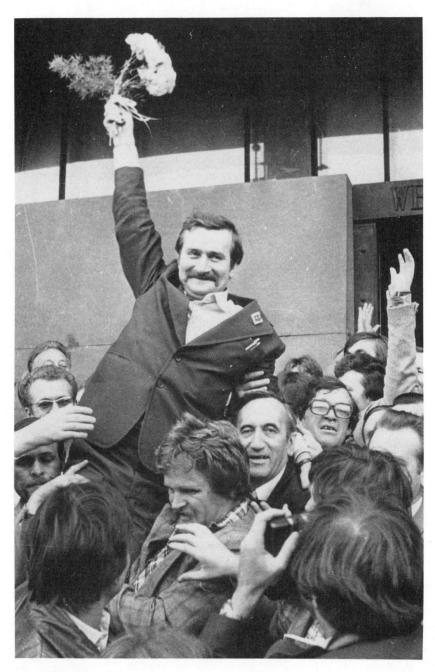

CHAPTER SEVEN

Lech Walesa: Organic Intellectual

The mode of existence of the new intellectual
can no longer consist of eloquence, the external
and momentary arousing of sentiments and passions,
but must consist of being actively involved in
practical life, as a builder, an organizer.

—ANTONIO GRAMSCI[1]

When Antonio Gramsci, one of the founders of the Italian Communist party, outlined his notion of the organic intellectual, he could not have imagined that over forty years later one of the best illustrations of his idea would be a Polish, Roman Catholic electrical engineer: Lech Walesa. But if Walesa exemplifies many of the qualities of Gramsci's worker-thinker, he also represents a transformation of Gramsci's ideal that reveals a new relationship among ideology, faith, and progressive politics.

For Gramsci, "every social class coming into existence creates with itself, organically, one or more groups of intellectuals who give it homogeneity and consciousness of its function—not only in the economic field but in the social and political fields as well."[2] These organic intellectuals are not to be confused with those who function as intellectuals in society—experts, professors, scientists, and administrators. These professionals seldom combine their techniques with "a humanist historical conception," and so most remain mere functionaries, never transcending their specialities to become leaders.

Nor is the organic intellectual to be confused with the literati and the other so-called "true intellectuals," who do not become mere functionaries but often remain politically ineffectual—addicted to books, ideas, and the psuedo-autonomy granted the intelligentsia that is, in effect, merely an excuse for inaction. The organic intellectual, in contrast to both these types, criticises life *and* works to change it.

But Gramsci's thinker-revolutionary was not going to be like Marx or Lenin, a thinker who had renounced the privileges and prestige of scholarly caste to identify with the revolutionary masses. Gramsci's thinker was to *emerge* from the working class as the embodiment of their needs, values, and concerns. He or she would live the unfolding historical dialectic, be educated to modern realities, and yet bring to bear upon these realities a critical point of view.

Gramsci remarks, "In the modern world, technical education, strictly tied to even the most primitive and unqualified industrial work *must* form the basis for the new type of intellectual."[3] For Gramsci, one is humanized and educated by labor. And in our industrial world, labor is organized on a variety of levels. Technical education clues one in to the hidden logic of the many layered industrial order. Once free to see the practical and economic rationale behind the complexities of modern living, one can begin to bring social realities into dialogue with a humanist historical conception. That is to say, one can then begin to think. Only to the degree one has seen through the one dimensional perspective common to the specialist-authorities, can the modern individual become a philosopher of the life she or he has received.

It is important here to point out that for Gramsci philosophy "cannot be reduced to a naturalistic anthropology; unity in mankind is not a quality of man's biological nature" but a point of arrival toward which the true thinker aspires through an active criticism of life.[4] The only true philosophy is "history in action, life itself,"[5] and, like the capitalists who transformed the feudal world largely due to the fact they were specialists in organizing production, the new organic intellectuals will transform the capitalist world largely because they are specialists in modern industrialization—people who grasp firsthand the links among technology, bureaucracy, production, and practical living because they are forced to forge those links every day on the job.

This forging of links is the *philosophical* side of what most workers today do for a living: they grease the economic machine, creatively resolving tensions and overcoming contradictions inherent in the world around them. They may be engineers trying to build quality goods in a socioeconomic context that demands cheap, but flashy, products or doctors seeking to heal in a world where their best efforts are often thwarted by economic and social contingencies. Whatever the case, today's technically educated professionals possess a proximity to the real problems of our day that makes them potential leaders of their class—provided the problems they face as workers can be brought into dialogue with a humanist historical conception and carried forward into a full-fledged criticism of life.

Lech Walesa clearly fits Gramsci paradigm for the new intellectual. He was technically educated as an engineer and acquired a humanistic conception of history through his participation in the Polish church—a church radicalized by the spirit of Emmanuel Mounier's personalism which had excited Polish Catholic intellectuals in Cracow during the 1930's—including Karol Wojtyla, later to become John Paul II.[6]

Walesa is not a scholar who renounced the privileges of his caste, but a worker who possesses no privileges to renounce. He is a plebeian reformer who wrestled moral leadership out of the hands of an already bureaucratized party apparatus led by "functional" party intellectuals. His values are not educated by the dialectic, but by the Church and by the ordinary brave man's resistance to the state philosophers. He identifies with the working class and says of himself: "For twenty-five years I was at the bottom. I was at the bottom, I am at the bottom, I will be at the bottom."[7]

Andrzej Drzycimski, a Polish writer, described Walesa's unique political genius in a way that reveals the character of the new working class in Poland.

> He addressed himself to the workers. But these were workers who belied the propaganda model in which they had been cast. Those to whom he spoke were educated and knew about the latest technical advances and about the country's problems. The fact that their sensibilities, their experience, their knowledge, their ability to conduct a dialogue and appreciate the general situation in the country were not recognized made them unwilling and reluctant to subscribe to the officially voiced slogans. Those seemed insincere to them. Speaking the truth openly, even the most painful truth, was Walesa's main objective and trump card.[8]

In other words, the official rhetoric of the party had lost touch with empirical historical realities—realities which were all too evident to the technically educated working class of Poland who were engaged in production and development. Walesa's great achievement was to voice this new worker's sensibility boldly and without compromise.

His impact upon the intellectuals of Poland has been profound. Volumes has been written about "The Walesa Phenomenon," sometimes with grudging admiration, but often with outright adulation for having brought off the cultural and national revival the intellectuals and artists of Poland had been preparing for years but which they could not themselves bring into being.

Walesa's own attitude toward intellectuals is slightly ambivalent. When greeted with the news that he has just been awarded an honorary doctorate from Cambridge, he asked suspiciously, "As who? As a worker?"[9] And although he has called on the writers and thinkers of his day to join in Solidarity, he has remarked that in the midst of a political struggle intellectuals take too long in their assessments of the historical context to be of much immediate value to the engaged politician. He complains that it takes intellectuals months to decide that he was right about a decision he had to make in fifteen minutes.

Some of this impatience, of course, is disingenuous. Walesa recognizes the need for expert analyses of the issues and has called for an advisory board of professionals to be formed to assist Solidarity in charting their future. But much of this impatience also represents the intuitions of an organic intellectual that there is a real difference between mere theory and real thinking. And that the psuedo-autonomy embraced by scholars often systematically distorts their perceptions, blinding them to the empirical realities of their age and the concerns of actual people. Upon receiving word that Walesa won the Nobel Peace Prize, his wife, Danuta, expressed this same working-class practicality when she remarked: "It's a great honor for the family. It's like a one-way ticket to history . . . perhaps one day the children will read a few lines about it in the encyclopedia. But will that be any good to them? They're still too young for this moment. They don't really understand what it means. On the other hand, they do know that their father is always busy and that each day that God gives them, they see precious little of him."[10]

One of the keys to the Walesa phenomenon may be that he is, in fact, a very simple man. Not simple intellectually. I have already argued that he represents the synthesis of a humanist historical conception with the practical perspective of the modern technician. But, rather, he is simple in the sense that he possesses an uprightness of soul that prevents self-consciousness, and this forthrightness allows him to expose the duplicity inherent in the official order virtually every time he opens his mouth. This is particularly evident in the simple and direct language of his speeches and interviews. Maria Janion put it this way:

> He (Walesa) would say—which instantly drew one's ears and attention to him—'Speaking for myself. . .' or 'Speaking for myself as a worker. . . .' The secret of his success began to reveal itself: it was above all the secret of his speech as the expression of his person and the expression of a community. He imprinted his stamp as someone who was saying exactly what he wanted to say. And nothing more. . .his way of speaking contained everything that led to his triumph. That he was able to be himself—a worker, a Pole, a Christian. That is the

best way to define the steps of his progress, from the particularism of a life in a job to a more universal level of culture.[11]

Walesa can speak powerfully because he is convinced of his own integrity, which is a different thing than being convinced of his abilities or of his moral superiority or even of his political ideals. Thus, he is open to negotiation, compromise, and new ideas, yet he is never so self-conscious as to weigh every word or action. His spontaneity is a function of his authenticity—a quality inherent in the organic intellectual and so often absent in traditional academics.

An example of Walesa's acceptance of his own fallibility and of the superiority of consensus politics can be seen in his response to the dramatic events of 1980 and the strike that established Solidarity as a national and international phenomenon.[12] Representing the shipyard workers, Walesa kept his demands simple: an increase in wages. When the authorities agreed under pressure from other sympathy strikes, Walesa accepted the agreement. Leaving the hall he held up his fist, announcing, "We won!" A colleague replied, "You've lost. You sold out all the other co-strikers for your own 2,000 zlotys per month victory." Aware of his blunder and the anger of the crowd, Walesa immediately reversed himself. "Then the strike's still on?" he both announced and inquired. "I will be the last to leave the yard!" Now, a less fickle, or should I say less existential, leader would have proceeded with much more theoretical consistency (or paralyzing self-doubt). But consistency was the least of Walesa's problems as he invented policies on the spot, reading the will of the people in the mood of the crowd, judging what was possible as it became possible, living on the unexpected as opposed to the preplanned. Such poverty of mind freed him to invent new positions in response to new realities because he did not identify with his own proposals.

But neither is Walesa so other-directed that he never turns a thought inward. He is not like those philosophically complacent American media politicians who float on the pleasant, the tangible, and the superficial, believing that the only real ideas are strategic ones. Walesa's spontaneity and faith in himself is built upon self-examination and the *insufficiency* of worldly values. He remarks,

> I fear only God—nobody else and nothing else. Apart from that, I am just a man who belongs to the time and the place he lives in, and tries to solve problems. I always believe there is a solution to each problem, even when everybody else says there is none.[13]

Walesa's faith is not a brand of positive thinking; it does not blind him to his own faults and limitations—it makes him more conscious of them in a way that does not paralyze him for action in the world but puts that action in its spiritual place. He remarks,

> I am always free, even when I am in prison! My thoughts, my dreams, my aspirations cannot be physically destroyed. The truth is always the truth. Christ lost physically as a man, but we now see that he won. Certainly I'm not measuring myself against him. I am a small fry.[14]

For Walesa, to lead, it is not necessary to command others, but to follow God. Faith can lift one out of history long enough to purge one of the petty progressive ideas of the day that dilute and confuse our quests for perfection. Thus faith centers Walesa's life, and his practical politics flow from that center outward. Unlike Lenin, who brought a global interpretation to bear on local realities, Walesa moves from the truth he perceives in local realities to their larger political implications. When questioned about the international impact of the Solidarity movement, he demurs saying only that he takes one step at a time, that it is too early to comprehend the global meaning of these events, and that right now there are smaller, more pressing, issues to be dealt with. The plebeian activist Walesa has no clearly formulated metasystem. His simple faith offers no clear refutation of the Polish state philosophers but rather lives on in such a way that its very existence testifies to a reality left out of the social equation.

Walesa often speaks of "the eyes" of the crowd—its visceral distrust—his awareness of its moods, its feeling life—and accepts the projections thrust upon him like a good psychotherapist: deflecting animosity and blame by reciprocating the identification and calling others to their own self-responsibility. By confronting the shadow self of his people in the hopes and fears they project upon him, he is capable of reading the Polish political scene like a psychoanalysis might read a dream: as a dramatic enactment of the self negotiating a zone of freedom between neurotically polarized alternatives. His job is to offer a creative interpretation that resolves the tensions by animating the will of the dreamer and, hence, generating hope. Walesa remarks:

> If I had to state what was the most valuable notion that helped me to deal with the complex reality of Poland from August 1980 onwards, I would say that it was being able to point to a third way in those situations where everybody says there are only two.[15]

This is a patient, developmental approach to solving social problems that rejects revolutionary violence but is no mere capitulation to the powers that be. It is not unlike Gandhi's perception that anger is best dealt with not by expressing it or repressing it—but experiencing it. And then acting in a manner that dignifies one's experience. In Walesa's case, this means that it does nothing to merely express or repress Poland's national resentments—either option only makes matters worse. But if someone in a leadership role like Walesa can articulate the experience of such resentments and yet still keep a cool head while attempting to institute just reforms, then the national neurosis ceases to eat away at the psyche of the people, and boundless new energy emerges from within the body politic. This is neither a utopian approach nor a merely realistic one; it blends elements of both, opting always for the third way.

During the years Solidarity was outlawed and Walesa was "absent" from the political scene, Poland's politics diversified. Opposition parties of both the left and right wings emerged with more extreme reform proposals than anything proposed by Solidarity. And yet by 1989 Solidarity remained the only real alternative to the Communist regime because it alone stood for consensus policies—not merely new ideas. Its continued popularity and global fascination derive not from its utopian aspirations, but from its honesty, its integrity, and its refusal to give up hope. This is enough of a utopia for a people tired of the lies and exaggerations of Marxist apologists and bureaucrats. And it is a model for the West as well, a West often so caught up in the pursuit of economic miracles that it has difficulty grasping how so poor a people might long as much for an end to hypocrisy as for an increase in material well-being. This is one of the reasons Western analyses of the Polish situation always seem so superficial, for although it is quite correct to give emphasis to economic issues, it is short-sighted to define everything in relationship to them. To do that is to flatten out history, to play the same one-dimensional game as the vulgar Marxists, and so to miss the real historical change taking place.

Lech Walesa has quoted the Polish sociologist Jan Strzelecki's analysis of the dynamics of Solidarity as a social movement:

> A certain kind of social demand is built up from below. If it is discovered that public money has been spent satisfying the elitist aims of a small group, this money must be recovered. We are dealing with both a movement of revolt and a motion to restore this country to its people. The same movement soon spreads into other domains: censorship, the way in which power is exercised, the principle of self-management in eco-

nomic activities. In this way we develop a new conception of the State: it is a State which no longer substitutes itself for the people but one which in carrying out its functions is served by a whole series of separate social organizations that together reflect an active society. A new actor appears on the national stage—the old show of "bogus participation" is over! All these elements constitute a whole that could eventually stand for something quite new if we could only find where its center of gravity lies.[16]

The aim of removing "bogus participation" is the goal of existentializing political life. And the center of gravity for this transformation, so far, has been Walesa himself—as the actual living embodiment of an engaged Polish citizen remaining true to his roots, his religion, and his national reponsibilities. This might explain Adam Michnik's remark, quoted in the New York Times Sunday Magazine in the fall of 1988, 'You know, our situation is unique in the Communist countries; Sakharov is interesting, but he is not a political alternative. Walesa is."[17]

When Solidarity took power in 1989, it did not represent a surreptitious bourgeois revolution or merely a move toward greater democracy on a national level. It represented a revolt within the Eastern bloc from the center of personal dignity outward to all four corners of the world. It represented the irresistible insistence that institutional forms should follow moral function. In fact, it represented the bold postmodern plebeian belief that the correct moral functioning of social institutions precedes their economic health.

It is a commonplace among Western journalists and commentators these days that Solidarity's triumph in 1989 is the beginning of the end of its influence—that as the opposition it enjoyed freedom from blame for insolvable economic ills, but now as part of the power structure it is also part of the problem. Its popularity will not survive harsh economic pains, pains unavoidable for any Polish government, Marxist or otherwise.

But these are the same people who thought Solidarity was dead when martial law was declared in December of 1981. Such analyses are more a reflection of the quick-fix mentality of Western style media politics. They totally underestimate the amount of moral pain the Poles have already had to endure, having lived as an occupied people for forty years. Moreover they underestimate the amount of patience, character, and resolve the people have accumulated as a result of these struggles. True, Solidarity is not, and never was, the majority in Poland. In 1976 there were only six members. But its values, as a human rights organization, have always transcended its numerical membership and have made it a transnational phenomenon almost from its inception. For Solidarity to succeed, it need not perform an economic miracle, but it must remain true to its own creative, honest, patriotic ways. The Polish people may not live up to such leadership, preferring to scapegoat their new representatives if things prove too difficult. But I doubt they will be so ungrateful or, for that matter, so self-destructive.

Jonathan Schell once remarked that not since the American Revolution have so many geniuses been collected in one small country at the same time.[18] And as such they offer, not merely a new government, but a new world-historic fix on things. In Walesa's book *A Way of Hope* (1987), this new fix on things comes through, not so much as a form of analysis, but as an affirmation of the common man and woman's political instincts. As I read the book, I found my own intuitions confirmed, and so my confidence in myself made stronger. It is as if, given the right moral coordinates, one can find one's own way out of any political forrest; but what is more, Walesa affirms that the compass for such navigation has been inside us all the time: we need only tap our own common decency and seek solidarity with others rather than advantage over them. The yardstick for progressive action is a simple one: what brings people together in common effort is good; that which divides them is bad.

Walesa's faith is a source of insight and strength, not mystification and authoritarianism, because it provides a way of articulating smothered human aspirations. It fuels resistance; it does not dampen it. The sacred offers individuals of faith a transvaluation of values, endowing them with intellectual freedom in a secular world beset by conflicting ideologies. Walesa remarks,

> I myself believe. I derive strength from faith, it is the motor of my life. I've always given public expression to it, but if anybody thinks differently I don't interfere. But during the strike, many people under those specific conditions, under permanent psychological stress, reminded themselves of the basic moral and ethical values with which they had been brought up. And that morality is sustained by the Church, which also spreads the truth. We lacked the truth at the time. Thus, we sought it in God's word as proclaimed by the Church. . . Many people understood then that what the Church has been saying for 2,000 years is the same thing we are fighting for.[19]

And what has the Church been saying for 2,000 years? We might say that it hasn't been very consistent. And yet let us not miss Walesa's point. What is has consistently stood for is a moral and spiritual dimension to life beyond the everyday go-round of material history. And it has stood for the idea that we can tap into that reality and move out from it into the world, transcending ourselves. Walesa's Catholicism does not demand that he follow a line, but that he invent a life, given the revelation of our divine responsibility to the good.

Walesa's Catholicism does not reduce to an ideology because it is based upon a mystery, which if properly understood is not something hidden but something revealed. That is to say, at the heart of his worldview is an image, not an idea; a metaphor, not a dogma; a drama, not a system. And though it can be said that metaphors indoctrinate in their own ways, it cannot be said that they do so in the same way or with the same rigor as other mere ideologies. Recent work on the linquistic qualities inherent in literary language, from the Russian formalists to the deconstructionists, make it abundantly clear that the mythopoetic core inherent in our religious traditions cannot be reduced to a logical system. Just as Gramsci contended that philosophy could not be reduced to naturalistic anthropology,[20] theology cannot be reduced to dogmatics, because it is as much a prophetic call to invent a life of integrity as it is a system of values.

Walesa's Catholicism by no means serves as the counterideology to Soviet Marxism. Rather it testifies to a mystery open to endless decipherment, application, and progress that cannot be grasped by secular state philosophers. As a system of images rather than a naturalistic anthropology, Christianity in Poland leads by prophetic inspiration. The parochial theology of the thirties—the theology Gramsci himself railed against and no doubt misinterpreted—has been superceded by a vision of the pastoral church that prefers to lead by example rather than by ecclesiastic fiat. Woe to any party or program that takes over that historically bankrupt function, and woe to anyone who reads the current doctrinal squabbles in the Church as an attempt to win it back. What went on at the synod in Rome, and what is going on in the streets of Poland, in the convents in the United States, and in the base communities in Latin America are experiments in living the faith that parallel the examinations of conscience religious souls constantly undergo.

Religion and politics are, in this sense, two of a kind. Unlike science or philosophy, they do not seek absolute truth so much as practical applications of received ideals. As a plebeian organic intellectual, Walesa does not look to philosophy as his guide to action; he looks to his conscience. But what conscience says is never self-evident. There are many deceptions that must be overcome through prayer, meditation, discussion, confession, the reading of scripture, and rational analysis. This process is something quite different than scientific inquiry or dialectical reasoning, which preserve the power of theoretical knowledge often at the expense of other ways of knowing and thus render null and void other significant aspects of human experience.

Thus Walesa embodies a more psychologically condensed version of the democratic values than that espoused by either Marx or the American founding fathers. When he talks about pluralism and self-determination, he is not talking about merely a bill of rights or a dictatorship of authentic proletariat social interests; he is talking about establishing the institutions and social values necessary for a life lived in accordance with conscience. And conscience demands self-critique, personal honesty, and a leadership that serves the people rather than manages them. Pluralism, in this sense, is not a code word for capitalist free-markets, but a way of overcoming the hegemony of the market mentality altogether.

The Walesa phenomenon may be a kind of political Rorschach test: one sees here the significance one wants to see. And admittedly much of Walesa's popularity in the West derives in part from the fact that he is such a convenient anti-soviet symbol. And yet the facts cannot be denied. One very unlikely electrical engineer has captured the imagination of the Western world and built a moral-cultural cosmos (Solidarity) our of a political choas. But what is even more startling is that he has done this without following any specific theoretical line. This is, perhaps, why he has been such a successful negotiator; his lack of ideological commitments keeps him intellectually mobile and unpredictable, while his religious faith keeps him aware of the scale and meaning of events. He remarks,

> I've met too many embittered people, politicians especially, who have been forced out of office and were obsessed with one overriding idea—their own—beside which nothing else counted, nothing else even existed. That is why I always find it difficult when people ask me what my theory is: what theory I identify with totally. To tell the truth, I don't identify myself with a theory at all. Not because I'm a skeptic, but because I'm a man of the soil, not the academy.[21]

And while Walesa admires the West for its economic success, he dislikes its emphasis on immediate material profit and its lack of long range vision.[22] As Solzhenitsyn put it in his Harvard address, "After the suffering of decades of violence and oppression, the human soul longs for things higher, warmer, and purer than those offered by to-day's mass living habits."[23]

In that same speech Solzhenitsyn went on to point out that even the youngest policy strategists in the Soviet Union laugh at our West-ern political wizards because their pragmatic policy proposals are not keyed to any commonly held historical overview and so not only do they lack any popular support, they are also shallow and without any firm philosophical ground. Walesa's practical political triumph comes in part from Solidarity's moral-historical critique of the Polish govern-ment. This larger philosophical framework allows Walesa to lose battles and yet still win wars; it sees past immediate problems to the larger values at stake. Walesa is not a tactician so much as a helmsman; he keeps the resistance on course.

Still Walesa cannot work miracles. Those who stand up to the state philosophers are still few in number. But he remains a symbol, a standard, and an icon for what is possible for the ordinary brave man who speaks out against the lie that history belongs to power, that honesty cannot prevail over worldly cunning, that faith is obsolete, and that our only defense against the totalitarian schemes that would re-duce us to statistical ashes is an equally brutal war of resistance purged of sentiment, grace, and conscience. On the contrary, Walesa's witness seems to tell us that without faith, resistance is doomed, and without conscience, triumph is impossible. It suggests that perhaps our best defense against totalitarian excess is a healthy distrust of positivist conceptions of history.

It seems that Soviet Marxism, read as the apotheosis of a strictly materialist humanism, has created its postmodern antitype in the the-oretically self-conscious ethnic counter cultures that are fighting for their very survival by living out transcendent philosophies. The mass cultures in the Western democracies, lacking any firm links to the eternities, fail to satisfy even their own populations' longings for heroic, saintly, and beautiful lives because they will not look the Prince in the eye, convinced that somehow they can avoid direct confrontation with evil through reason, technology, and progress. But at some time each of us recognizes the hollowness of this promise and believes that some-where, somehow we are called to be brave. Our short-term pragma-tism denies us the opportunity most of the time, and so our emotional lives degenerate into sentimentalism and cynicism while our character atrophies and our culture is replaced by entertainment and efficency oriented therapies.

Walesa, by contrast, dared to look the Prince in the eye, and to the world's surprise, the Prince blinked. But let us not confuse heroism with victory. Walesa may yet find himself caught in a clash between the humanistic values of Solidarity and the dirty devices necessary to realize those values in history. To refuse the latter for the former is, in one sense, to insure worldly failure, and Walesa may yet become a martyr for moderation in an age of excesses. But as of today it seems he will probably avoid these fates. His capacity to embrace doubt, to risk, to move forward into ever-deeper waters, and to trust his gut, his goodness, and his God, bespeaks a new kind of politics, a politics one might well describe as plebeian postmodernism.

Chapter Eight

The Modernization of Poverty, Stupidity, and Family Life: Shared Rejections

*The religious lunacy which worships the God of
philosophers and bankers would indeed justify us in
proclaiming that God is dead, if indeed that idol
were he. Could we only have a little respite from
the wars, to carry on with our technical miracles,
then glutted with comfort we should then be able to
declare that happiness was dead. Another
fourteenth century, as it were, crumbling away
before our eyes: the time for "a second Renaissance"
is at hand.*

—Emmanuel Mounier[1]

From a plebeian perspective, modernity has been a mixed blessing. It has generated new wealth and created a much less brutish
physical existence for many. But at the same time, the new technologies have generated new needs and with them new ways to be
needy. Moreover, they have transformed all the old plebeian vices into
new, more virulent strains and rendered many of the old plebeian
virtues obsolete.

Modernization can make anyone who cannot afford something as
tangibly remote as car insurance an economic nonentity—virtually
expelled from any active participation in the culture at large. And,
as Ivan Illich has argued, many new technologies have taken away
the value of traditional skills such as walking or independent thinking.[2] Other plebeian virtues such as sincerity and loyalty may, in
fact, make one vulnerable to the new technologies of marketing
and salemanship—or at least incapable of being employed in these
industries.

And there are countless other examples of the disutilities generated by technological progress. Illich estimates—taking the amount of
time the average American spends dealing with cars per year and
dividing it by the number of miles traveled—our average speed as

drivers equals less than 5 miles per hour.[3] An advance hardly worth dismantling the landscape and transforming our entire economy and culture to accomplish. He also points out that although medical costs have skyrocketed, infant mortality rates and longevity figures have not improved appreciably in the last ten years.

These negative side-effects of our technological civilization are beginning to sour the ordinary individual's view of the grandiose claims for technological progress. But the pervasiveness of these side effects and their basis in the economic infrastructure of an increasingly global system of industrial development has resulted in a cynical public acceptance of them as necessary evils. And although the total set of discrete personal outrages is mounting every day—from deteriorating cities, endless commutes, and overpriced housing, to deteriorating schools, minds, and national culture—the average person feels helpless to do anything about it, as if swept away by a great tide of the inevitable desanctification and trivialization of her or his own experience.

If there is little intrinsic worth to anything outside its function within an ever-changing market, and if the market itself is built upon the a priori rejection of all humanist assumptions and moral restraints, then everything becomes a commodity, and nothing is sacred. Couple this with the fact that one's sentimentality and most superficial sexual appetites are continually affirmed by the media as an expression of penultimate value, and you have a formula not only for perpetual alienation but for a society driven by the concretized abstractions of a crazed economic system and, thus, totally out of touch with reality.

This postmodern wasteland has its sources in three paradoxical developments:

> 1. A perpetual revolution of economic life that generates endless new individual needs and endless new poverties—laying waste to the planet's ecology at the very moment it generates vast new social wealth (capital)
>
> 2. An increasingly managed information system centered around a mass media that exalts received ideas over direct experience—creating in the process pseudo-environments and modernized stupidity disguised and given credibility through the sheer pervasiveness of their presence
>
> 3. A disintegrated and dispirited family life increasingly powerless to protect its members against the cultural hegemony of an economically driven world-system that sentimentalizes interpersonal values—thereby destroying their revolutionary potential by rendering them the private property of

alienated individuals instead of the solid ground upon which universal human solidarity might be built

The difficulty ordinary people face in defending themselves against these trends is that these trends have, in fact, freed them from many of the traditional burdens of everyday life. What is new is that people are beginning to ask, At what cost? And they are searching their own spiritual traditions for answers.

In his fascinating little treatise *The Red Book and the Great Wall* (1968), Alberto Moravia reflects upon his visit to China during the cultural revolution. He found a nation in poverty—traditional poverty—but liberated from "the superfluous." He doubted that this essential life could last and predicted a less utopian future for China after modernization reinstates the resentments, ambitions, and general unhappiness of a society divided by rich and poor. So long as poverty is normalcy, he commented, it is not dehumanizing.

And then he makes this remarkable prophecy:

> One day common people, endowed with common sense, are going to get bored with being inhuman or, rather, with being continually dehumanized by wealth. And they will get rid of it, even if philosophers and producers of the superfluous swear that they are wrong.[4]

Is it so unthinkable that a civilization after hundreds of years of overproduction could decide to move in a different direction—working less, reflecting more, living simply? Perhaps Gandhi, Mother Teresa, and their precursors Thoreau and Tolstoy are not textbook eccentrics after all but harbingers of this dawning postindustrial, postproduction, postmodern epoch where life is lived free from the organized mirage—the programmed phantasmagoria—of commercial civilization. For Gandhi the spinning movement "broke" with the monopoly of industrial production and affirmed the link between who we are and what we do. For Mother Teresa voluntary poverty breaks the cycle, exposes the consumption "trance," and affirms use values.

One of the most puzzling scenes for Western viewers of Ann and Jeanette Petrie's film *Mother Teresa*[5] occurs when Mother Teresa is inspecting a new shelter donated to the Sisters of Charity in San Francisco. The Sisters find the building a bit "too nice" for their purposes, and so proceed to rip out the carpeting and toss it in a dumpster in the alley below. This seeming act of gratuitous self-mortification is actually an act of solidarity and identification with the poor. By choosing to live in poverty, one breaks its spell as an index of self-worth. In throwing out the carpet, one is affirming one's independence from production values.

But it isn't just poverty that wears a new face since modernization; so do our habits of thought and our intellectual vices. In his "Jerusalem Address: The Novel and Europe," Milan Kundera claims that one of Flaubert's greatest achievements as a novelist was to document the progress of stupidity. Traditional stupidity was simple ignorance. One did not know, and one knew one did not know, but one could find out. Science, technology, schools, and the media, however, did not eliminate stupidity—they transformed it. Now stupidity is not simple ignorance but "the non-thought of received ideas."[6] It is a much more dangerous phenomenon than its predecessor because it masks itself as intelligence and real knowledge.

Today after watching television news the average citizen feels capable of voicing opinions on world-historical events that no serious scholar would even pretend to understand. Gone is any sense of the difficulty of thought or the need to earn the right to certain ideas. The direct knowledge the premodern world was built upon has been replaced by a simulacrum of understanding. When H. L. Mencken defined education as the art of throwing phoney pearls before real swine, he was describing the role our schools play in the modernization of stupidity. Much of our crisis in education comes from not owning up to these new forms of inanity our culture has produced—especially its blurring of boundaries between high and popular culture. Many theoreticians of the postmodern see this confusion of realms as evidence of some lasting ontic shift, when in fact it may simply be evidence of our growing failure to make intellectual distinctions.

Dietrich Bonhoeffer noted this same "coming of age" of stupidity in his essay on folly.[7] Convinced that Nazism was no simple historical anomaly, but a sign of the times, he tried to comprehend how otherwise seemingly intelligent and sane people could fall under its sway. He decided that it was a sociological phenomenon—a species of folly— the psychological product of the modernization of information technologies. It's not that human intellectual capacities have been diminished, but the sheer pervasiveness of collective opinion is so vast that individuals simply give up trying to assess things for themselves— after all, everybody already knows what's happening already, don't they? Why struggle to invent a map of the world when the media glove-compartment offers you thousands of ready-mades?

This new stupidity is particularly virulent in middle-class professionals. Convinced they must know something because they are making money, have a degree, or have mastered a set of techniques, they proceed to interpret the social world based upon the self-evident absolutes of received ideas. Solzhenitsyn has even commented upon the influence of this class within the Soviet Union:

> An educated petite bourgeoisie has grown up throughout the industrialized world—(Yes, Indeed!) And what a horrible class it is, this immense stratum of shoddily educated mediocrities, this educated rabble which has usurped the title of intelligentsia—of the geniune creative elite, which is always very small in number, and individualistic through and through. This educated rabble includes the whole party apparat.[8]

The historical role of the middle class has been to stand in the way of their own imaginative lives—affirming surety at the cost of ontological vibrance, seeking their own material well-being before intellectual or moral excellence. For them the big lie has been that they have it all—when, in fact, the most sensitive among them are engaged in a search for essential life that is hopeless. Money dominates their lives, and in their better moments they will admit that they have never lived comfortably with this truth. So, like their Romantic and Victorian precursors, they engage in a rearguard action to preserve a sense of themselves as a cultured elite; but such self-deception just doesn't wash, given the enormity of their ignorance.

This self-doubt makes them prey to political con-artists and commercial "visionaries" who sell dreams without inspiring the discipline necessary for self-mastery. Co-opted middle-class plebeians become petite-bourgeois consumers—systematically miseducated, underestimated, physically pampered, and morally exploited. They are the hollow men celebrated by the media as free spirits for whom anything is possible, while their actual personal histories, ethnicity, personality, and moral seriousness have been marginalized, if not entirely wiped out, by the the powers that be. They are energized only by the niggardly self-improvement schemes that constitute what passes for their cultural lives.

Postmodern plebeians like Lech Walesa and Mother Teresa, recognizing the emptiness of most of what passes for thought these days, have refused to identify with the educated classes or the cultural avantgarde, which has led to their appearing anti-intellectual. But their suspicion of ideas comes from their recognition that in our age of "modernized stupidity," social criticism, however trenchant, can become an instrument of folly unless the idols that pervert it and the systems that distort it are not first dismantled.

Modern stupidity has a certain resistance to critique; it ignores it only to absorb it in its own ironic attitudes and poses. But rather than despair over this, postmodern plebeians move courageously to assault the concrete embodiments of such distorted perceptions through direct action: building hospices that try to restore some dignity to death, mounting campaigns against racism, befriending the lonely and the outcast, and working on themselves through spiritual disciplines that force them to resist the dissolution of their own moral consciousness.

For Bonhoeffer, the folly of the new stupidity could not be overcome by instruction, but only by an act of liberation—a personal transformation that leads the individual to aspire to a responsible life before God as opposed to a successful life within the cultural trance.[9] And although outward liberation from economic pressures is often required before the inner transformation can take place, Marxist dialectics cannot in and of itself overcome folly because it too is primarily a form of instruction, a method, a heuristic as available to self-serving individuals as any other instrument or tactic. Its very rationality and impersonality make it as powerful for the corrupt as for the virtuous. Authentic progressive social action cannot be based upon such instrumentalities— the means and the end must be one. This was the great Gandhian insight!

As a plebeian absolute, the state of the family also serves as an index of the effects of modernity on the ordinary person. In its systems and dysfunctions we can see what has happened to the traditions of the deep self and read the virtues and vices of our times. Less a socializing tool or economic force than it had been in the agricultural age, the modern family has become a kind of shadow culture, an underground for private existence that is raided by outside systems of commerce and government for economic support and political assent.

For the most part, modern families' defenses against these incursions are so weak that their members gladly identify with the less demanding role models and myths the commercial culture provides for them, leading them to reject the often time-consuming and laborious work of building and healing relationships over time. Mother Teresa put it this way:

> Everybody today seems to be in such a terrible rush, anxious for greater developments and greater riches and so on, so that children have very little time for their parents. Parents have very little time for each other, and in the home begins the disruption of the world.[10]

When we look at the statistics on divorce, alcoholism, addiction, mental illness, and child abuse, we come to the inescapable conclusion that families are not sources of stability for ordinary people so much as psychological battlegrounds where individuals fight for their sanity against great odds. At its worst, family life has become a strange preserve of passions, addictions, compulsions, persecutions, and codependencies: the church of dependent bourgeois love. In the nineteen sixties, R. D. Laing in *The Politics of Experience* (1967), described family life this way:

> The family's function is to repress Eros; to induce a false consciousness of security; to deny death by avoiding life; to cut off transcendence; to believe in God, not to experience the Void; to create, in short, one-dimensional man; to promote respect, conformity, obedience; to con children out of play; to induce fear of failure; to promote respect for work; to promote a respect for respectability. [11]

Laing's modernist critique exposed the alienating fiction of our social selves and the family's role in generating it. But today we would worry about setting anyone free in a culture that has many other more effective tools for socializing—and hence alienating, the individual—than just Dad and Mom. If the family represses Eros, the consumer culture exploits it and demeans it, repressing other human qualities such as moral intelligence. There are no bourgeois-free zones anymore—not even in the imagination; we are all born into reductive, class ridden ambitions and identities as thick as Exxon sludge.

Writing in the nineteen twenties, Sinclair Lewis expressed the modernist impatience with the self-preoccupations of bourgeois family life this way:

> What I fight in Zenith is standardization of thought, and, of course, the traditions of competition. The real villains of the piece are clean, kind, industrious Family Men who use every known brand of trickery and cruelty to insure the prosperity of their cubs. The worst thing about these fellows is that they're so good, and in their work at least, so intelligent. You can't hate them properly, and yet their standardized minds are the enemy. [12]

The workaholics described by Lewis represent dysfunction. Playing roles and assuming grandiose responsibilities are not essential requirements of family life. Families need not be so alienating, bourgeois or duplicitous; they can and should be enpowering—connecting us to a realm of intimacy inaccessible through less permanent relationships.

Tolstoy's vision of the relationship between Kitty and Levin in *Anna Karenina* expresses this kind of healing love, as does Antonio Machado in his poem "Si yo fuera un poeta,"

> I know your eyes do not answer mine,
> they look and do not question when they look:
> your clear eyes, your eyes have
> the calm and good light,
> the good light of the blossoming world, that I saw
> one day from the arms of my mother.[13]

As a source of transcultural experience the family has long been a plebeian value and ideal; but it never could manifest itself at its best in simple conformity to bourgeois norms. To get there one must practice domestic satyagraha and creative suffering.

But if one can manage the internal dynamics of projection and one's own susceptibility to role playing—families can be counter-hegemonic forces preserving the individual conscience against the alienation produced by society at large. At their best they can be preserves of intimacy, disclosure, forgiveness, self-discovery, and renewal.

But the institutions of family life we have inherited have been badly damaged by the forces of industrialization that separated domestic values from economic worth and by the media that have sentimentalized, and thereby dispirited, family life, turning it into some kind of transgenerational hobby requiring snapshots, group vacations, and all the other accountrements of a thriving Victorian theatrical production. And it has been hurt by its own premodern residual resistance to, what Jung called, "individuation." Families still choose to define themselves as institutional entities, rather than as countercultural forces for personal and social reform.

Robert Bly described the psychological dynamic at the heart of modern family life this way:

> While the bride and groom stand in front of the minister exchanging rings, another exchange takes place in the basement. During a separate meeting, the mother passes over the son's witch, which she has been carrying to the bride. An hour after the ceremony it is firmly in place inside the bride, though it will take a while to show up, because neither the bride, not the mother, nor the groom knows about this second ceremony. . . .a similar exchange takes place between the groom and the bride's father. . .The bride's father passes over to the groom as much as he can find of the giant or the tyrant

that he has been carrying for his daughter. The bride's father leaves the church door lighter, the groom heavier.[14]

I suspect that a similar exchange takes place after the first child is born, only this time the child receives the mother's hero projections and/or the father's goddess projections. As a result both father and mother leave the hospital lighter but weaker while the child becomes the power center of the home. These projections in a postmodern setting cause us to feel the weight of family life as the antithesis of what Kundera has called "the incredible lightness of being." History, economics, and society itself seem almost painless veneers—Disneylands of possibilities—compared to the deep, brooding, inescapable realities of family life. In the industrialized world the anonymous self can trip the urban fantastic in a drama of self-making, where personal projects are inflated to the grandiose proportions of a large-screen television, and thereby never brought into conflict with limiting moral obligations and so never really suffered through. But in a marriage the unconscious is an inescapable, palpable presence.

In *A Little Book on the Human Shadow* (1988), Robert Bly uses a Jungian metaphor to describe how we empower our spouses with our own projected vices. Men, he claims, often project their "witchy" attributes onto their mothers and then onto their wives, refusing to contribute anything to the feeling life of the household, wearing a kind of put-upon "nice guy" persona, unwilling to express, or unable to express, any concrete needs or desires. Such men often give in to their wife's seeming willfulness. The wife, for her part, finds herself strangely taking on the witchy attributes of her husband's projections almost in spite of herself, often projecting her own "tyrant" traits onto the man. To win back the balance within the family and within the individual psyches, a kind of domestic satyagraha must take place. Bly suggests that husbands go to their wives and ask for their witch back. And then they should turn to the side and eat it in a symbolic ritual act, absorbing into their own consciousness their own implacable self-will instead of projecting it upon all the women in their lives. The wife, for her part, must ask for her tyrant back.[15]

For Gandhi, good families model the good society. And regardless of what one might think of the particulars of Bly's analysis of American domestic politics, there is a recognition here that the self-responsibility fostered by nonviolent confrontation is one of the keys to a happy household. It condenses us psychologically and so frees others from codependent reactions to us, allowing them to discover and express their own independent values. Families are one of the few laboratories of such heightened self-making left to us, and so their preservation is not so much a nostalgia as a practical way of staying in touch with certain otherwise inaccessible life energies.

Family life, then, is a residual plebeian idealism that is fading fast but dying hard. In its everyday pain, it testifies to another kind of living and another form of responsibility that the utilitarian minds of comfort-seeking moderns cannot comprehend. It is becoming less and less a refuge from the world and more and more its stark antithesis. Its joys are of a different order than pleasure, always tinged with the melancholy awareness of failure, of death, of passing time.

And so all marriages are, in a sense, "religious," because the deep selves they affirm are essentially mystical. Ultimately it is the metaphysical aspect of one's spouse that one marries, not their ever changing and changeable attributes. In a post-Christian world, marriage, like hypocrisy, is a kind of tribute vice pays to virtue. It is a leap into the traditions of the deep self that most make unknowingly. In such an environment, divorce becomes the more meaningful existential act because it is a choice and not a blind leap. And yet the "fated" quality of marriage, the sense that it is a product of forces greater than oneself, is its greatest asset, preserving a sense of destiny, mythological depth, and meaning in a world where our choices are—let us admit it— primarily a menu of disingenuous escapist options.

In one of his marriage homilies, Bonhoeffer told the new couple that their love had brought them to marriage, now they were to let their marriage bring them to love. I think he was trying to express family life as an inward turning requiring a different kind of love. A love born after and through commitment. A love on the other side of love.

In a recent interview Elie Wiesel was asked how he would like to be remembered. He replied, "As a Jew, naturally. As a witness. As a good father."[16] They are quite similar vocations, and growing closer together every day. Each is a fate that, once accepted, becomes a destiny. Each affirms love despite love's sorrow. Each is an act of faith.

These three developments—the modernization of poverty, of stupidity, and of family life—have made it difficult for ordinary people to gain access to the wisdom of their traditions and cultures of origin. In the United States, "plebeians" are the alienated souls of much modern fiction, caught up in what Octavio Paz once described as a prosperity without grandeur and a hedonism without risk.[17] It is hard for them to even define the terms of their own psychological displacement. They are the Martha Quests, the running rabbits, the invisible men and minimalist anti-heroes of contemporary fiction—hopelessly in love with virtue but incapable of achieving it. Although privileged, they feel exploited. Although comforted, they are trivialized; free but diminished.

This restlessness leads plebeians to cling to religious values as a stay against their own economic and ethical obsolescence. Plebeians assert the existence of the inner life and the deep self, honor achievement as an ethical accomplishment, and believe in humanity—hoping to carry it forward into the next century—not on the backs of the Third World or in the supersonic transports of the ruling elite—but on the wings of individual accomplishments. To do this, however, requires a new assessment of the plebeian's role in the scheme of things that links their spiritual aspirations to a social critique.

This is difficult because they find themselves torn by two competing destinies: assimilation into the modern order or resistance against the desanctification of the world. This is the great plebeian issue of whether or not one has sold out, and it is the source of tensions between what used to be called "hip" and the "square" lives—a tension Mailer describes so poignantly in his essay "The White Negro."[18] The long history of boosterism in the public life of the United States is a record of the attempt to step over this problematic by absorbing the "perfection" of personhood within the larger "ignorance" of the market. But this blatant play to the plebeian vices has never been a real option to individuals of character or conscience. And so the subjective lives of contemporary plebeians have become one of the key arenas where the dramatic struggle to redescribe our age is taking place. Just as breaking the monopoly of the party is the plebeian project in Eastern Europe, overcoming the hegemony of the market is the plebeian project in the West.

The more powerful one's subculture with its own countermythology, the more difficult it is to give oneself over to the commercial standards of each succeeding "new age." This is no doubt why some of our most eloquent expressions of the plebeian sensibility come from ethnic minorities—people like Toni Morrison, Ishmael Reed, Bernard Malamud, Alice Walker, and Maxine Hong Kingston. For them, modernity was never about the transcendence of myth; it was always about myths in conflict. For them it is not the disappearance of the deep self that characterizes the drama of our times, but its strategies for survival.

Plebeians are forever the odd man out; unlike Fanon's wretched of the earth, they cannot find their dignity and historic role unified in revolution. And yet their spiritual longings compel plebeians to seek more than the status quo. This quest for an impossible universe embodies Camus's notion of the absurd with a vengeance. But plebeians resist Camus's articulate existential description of their aspirations—preferring instead the mythical and religious language of their ancestors. The mass-media marketers understand the conservative spiritual longings of the plebeian mind all too well and so produce popular fictions that substitute the comforting illusion of a paradise achieved for the heroics demanded for authentic reform. But the longings of the plebeian soul cannot be so easily assuaged by the manufactured myths of the Hollywood pastoral. There is a hunger for greatness within the ordinary soul that is languishing under the patronizing self-promotions of our commercial culture. Somehow we know that the truth that heals is the truth that hurts, and yet without leadership we flinch at the sacrifices needed to achieve it.

CHAPTER NINE

Plebeian Postmodernism: Shared Affirmations

*Living unreservedly in life's duties, problems,
successes and failures, experiences and perplexities.
In so doing we throw ourselves completely into the
arms of God, taking seriously, not our own
sufferings, but those of God in the world—watching
with Christ in Gethsemane. That I think is faith,
that is metanoia; and that is how one becomes a
man and a Christian.*

—DIETRICH BONHOEFFER[1]

A new ethic has walked unexpectedly onto the stage of world
history looking very much like an ordinary person. Clothed in prison
fatigues from Buchenwald and the Soviet gulag, in a Polish workshirt
and homespun cloth from Calcutta, this ethic has already toppled governments and reconciled what was once thought irreconcilable. It expresses itself through the concrete deeds of simple people who insist
on finding their own bearings in history without sacrificing their integrity or personal sense of the sacred.

As yet these new champions of the people have no name. Nonetheless, we see them everywhere—in Poland, Czechoslovakia, China,
Tibet, and South Africa—ordinary people committed to the spiritual
traditions that have defined their cultures. As such, their victories
represent something more and other than merely the triumph of populist reform movements; they are part of a legacy of personal virtue that
runs like an underground stream beneath the great violent expanse of
world history.

In the West, we are tempted to read the political changes sweeping across the world as evidence of the triumph of democracy, progress,
and rationality over the antireligion of messianic Marxism, especially
when celebrated Chinese dissidents, like Fang Lizhi, refer to the communist leadership as "feudal lords." But looking at the lives and the
works of Gandhi, King, Solzhenitsyn, and Walesa, we can see that

there is much more to Solidarity than anticommunism, more to non-violence than bloodless power-shifts, and more to the critiques of Soviet state hegemony than an attack upon Stalinism. At the core of these developments is a new traditionalism and respect for the old ways. The real innovation here is the bold application of plebeian religious values to postmodern political circumstances—the insistence by each of these figures that the person matters, that the sacred exists, and that God exists not as the foundation of the world but as the ultimate trope against the will to power, the will to define, the fascistic urge to totality.

It is, of course, too early to tell whether an authentic politics of the sublime will come out of all this—a politics that actually leads to the realization of exquisite human possibilities. But if such a reality is ever to emerge, the policies that shape it will have to come from people like those examined here, people who understand that the real issues of our day are not simply economic development and modernization but the problematics of assimilation, the diminished inner-lives of private individuals, and the fate of the earth.

Taken together the six figures considered here move us closer, if not to a resolution of these issues, at least to a greater understanding of their dynamics. Their key shared insight is that thinking cannot be reduced to naturalistic philosophy, that human unity is not a given but a destination, that the only true philosophy is, as Gramsci put it, "history in action, life itself." Hannah Arendt expressed this same idea when she wrote that "thought itself rises out of incidents of living experience and must remain bound to them as the only guideposts by which to take its bearings."[2] In other words, truth is always practical, contextual, individual; while theory is derivative, and the will to a system, a lack of integrity.

Under a global market economy, the practical reason of ordinary people is largely subsumed within an amalgam of money-making projects and development schemes. There is no direct commercial pay-off to thinking philosophically and so no reason to be intellectually engaged beyond the demands of technological innovation. There are many roles to play (some call them opportunities to be seized) and very little incentive to seek an essential self or pose a critical standard. In other words, insofar as practical life is the zone where history and philosophy meet, plebeians living within a market system that lays claim to absolute reality have very little reason to be practical in the old philosophical sense of that word. They are too busy working, making money, serving the dreams of capital. Their fantastic lives, especially if they are successful, may strike them as dreams come true when they are more truly programmed fantasmorgoria, fictive constructs tailor-made to serve the ends of the prevailing commercial interests.

Plebeians are, therefore, cut off from any sense of transcendence or the sublime.

The modern economic order regulates this diminishment of being through its assertion of a totalizing naturalistic philosophy that reassures those who live within it that the progress of the whole redeems any personal demoralization they may be experiencing; it reassures them that their sacrifice of traditional personal virtue, their sacrifice of the past, the heroic, the essential self, is—from a global perspective—not only economically necessary, but politically redemptive.

The message of the six plebeian activists examined here argues *exactly the opposite view*—that if we are to ever achieve what we want—and what we want is sacred life—then practical life must become philosophic again and thereby resist the obsolence of the deep self by reinterpreting everyday experience as a series of opportunities through which to realize sublime ends. Any notions of totality—either Marxist or market inspired—must be given up in order to enter into the concrete existential obligations that allow us to live once again within sacred time. By reanimating the creative power of our own indigenous traditions, these plebeian reformers affirm our individual longings for holy existence. Mother Teresa put this willingness to enter into a future free from roles and totalizing rationales this way:

> We must not attempt to control God's actions. We must not count the stages in the journey he would have us make. We must not desire a clear perception of our advance along the road, nor know precisely where we are on the way of holiness. I ask him to make a saint of me, yet I must leave to him the choice of that saintliness itself and still more the choice of the means which lead to it.[3]

Consciousness-raising efforts and material reforms are superficial palliatives that simply can't undo the triumph of the inessential. What is needed is a revolution of heart, a revolution in values and sentiment, culminating in the birth of a new man and new woman who are, in fact, the old man and old woman, purged of hubris and ambition. Reconciled to their limitations, but elevated by a desire to serve, they live on love. Or rather it would be more accurate to say love lives on in them—in the psychological space they provide merely by erasing all that psychological content that makes modern neurotics so productive, fascinating and complex. For the plebeians examined here, politics ought to be subsummed within practical spirituality and become an aspect of character formation, part of the puzzle of the self, not a tragic fate or an alien imposition on our natural lives.

Of course, there are other insights to be derived from this new plebeian perspective, but for the sake of clarity and focus let me point out what I consider to be the seven key lessons.

The First Lesson

The first lesson of plebeian postmodernism is that our real self is our moral self. And the moral self is a second self. That is to say, the moral self is not a birthright or a natural outgrowth of education or conditioning; it is an individual accomplishment requiring risk and creative suffering. As Octavio Paz put it in *The Labyrinth of Solitude*, "To be oneself is always to become that other person who is one's real self, that hidden promise or possibility."[4] To be a person, in other words, is to have a vocation, to respond to a call; it means living for something more important than prosperity. It requires a re-identification with the best in oneself, which is to say, a re-identification with the progressive forces of one's own culture of origin.

History is not a blank slate. We are born into complex circumstances and deep obligations that define us more powerfully and completely than we can ever know. But this need not be a burden to those plebeian souls who by discovering their ancestors, their progeny, and their sacred responsibilities come to know themselves. It links the plebeian to a story larger than that of her or his own personal life. This story calls them to a life of gratitude and transcendence. The larger humanity of this historicized self inspires them to seek a more difficult but more exquisite existence for themselves than they ever could have imagined on their own. Martin Luther King defined this sublime vision of human possibility starkly, but correctly, when he remarked that "an individual has not started living until he can rise above the narrow confines of his individualist concerns to the broader concerns of all humanity."[5]

Solzhenitsyn equates the attainment of this second self as the birth of one's own unique point of view—a distinct, independent perspective "more precious than life itself." But he makes it clear that such an achievement occurs within one's historical context. For example, upon attaining such a perspective, Nerzhin, who is Solzhenitysn's main character in *The First Circle*,

> . . . understood the people in a new way, a way he had not read about anywhere: the people is not everyone who speaks our language, nor yet the elect marked by the fiery stamp of genius. Not by birth, not by the work of one's hands, not by the wings of education is one elected into the people.

But by one's inner self.

Everyone forges his inner self year after year.

One must try to temper, to cut, to polish one's soul so as to become *a human being.*

And thereby become a tiny particle of one's own people.[6]

To achieve a moral perspective on existence, Solzhenitsyn contends, you cannot begin with some concretized abstraction such as the people from which to derive an ethic. Rather you must begin with your own personal (even sectarian) point of view and then work to enlarge its sympathies.

James Baldwin called this existential vantage point "the view from here," and considered it to be the necessary, if limited, starting point for any exposition of the truth. It represents the theoretically self-conscious affirmation of the detranscendentalized subject to his or her partial, but nonetheless actual, participation in world-historic realities. "The view from here" represents a radically historicized common sense grounded in the concrete particulars of everyday experience and refined through creative suffering. It is free of the theoretical hubris of the dialectical imagination. It resembles the thought before history (myth) and the thought outside of history (mysticism), and yet it is neither, because its main concern is with particular concrete events in all their manifest historicity and "lost" promise.

The Plebeian Pastoral

The second lesson follows directly upon the first, for once one attains this second self and answers the call to witness for a more inclusive humanity, one immediately comes into conflict with the untransformed world. In the lives of our six exemplary plebeians, this clash often gives rise to events that dramatize the gross disproportion between simple virtue and an increasingly complex world system that has gone beyond the negative implosion of philosophical nihilism to, in many instances, actual despair and terrorism. As a result the plebeian postmodern pastoral does not reveal the pseudosophistication of city life as did the premodern pastoral so much as testify to a saving remnant of actual hope persevering on the streets and in the concentration camps.

Postmodern plebeians are not unself-conscious exemplars of virtue but possess theoretical self-consciousness of their role as representatives of countercultural values. Moreover, they do not resist the dual consciousness this self-awareness provokes in them, but try to move beyond cultural alienation to an acceptance of their roles as displaced reformers, recognizing their need for metaphors, masks, roles, and fictions, as survival tools. This trickster mentality can be seen in Solzhenitsyn's celebration of zek survival strategies, which do not always adhere to the law, and in Walesa's reputation as an unpredictable negotiator willing to abandon any position immediately if he thinks he has been maneuvred into a compromising stance. One sees this dualconsciousness in the theatre of Gandhian protest, in Martin Luther King donning a new pair of stiff, blue Levis on his way to be arrested, and even in the modest self-consciousness of a Mother Teresa, who upon emerging blood-splattered from a delivery room, once happily remarked, "Our Loreto nuns should see this!"[7]

In this sense, postmodern plebeianism is a kind of satirical pastoral, ironically aware of its own dramatic excesses but embracing them anyway as the only option from which to generate reform. It is an assertion of moral presence that is neither self-righteous nor ameliorist because it is above all other things self-critical and exegetical. That is to say, postmodern plebeianism generates its values not through system building or ideology but through tropes upon what Foucault called the prevailing "regime of truth."

At the opening of Luis Valdez's play *Zoot Suit* the narrator tells us that it was the dream of every vato inside and outside the barrio to don the Zoot Suit and play the myth![8] The adolescent dream of a new life represents here the vital intuitive recognition by ghetto youth of their need to remake themselves, to link up to mythic, archaic energies transcending their public roles and social predicament. We could argue about which myth might best serve their liberation and whether the Zoot Suiter was a commendable model, but he did represent a conscious reidentification with one's people. He had found a way to be reborn. And this was an inspiring accomplishment. Everyone, especially the Zoot Suiter himself, knew it was a phoney identity, a fantasy, a play, but it was a consciously chosen play, not the unconscious, habituated life of the bourgeoisie, or the demeaning Mexican sterotypes imposed by the majority culture.

The problem here, of course, is that this energizing myth of radical self-assertion is precisely the appeal of fascism. The Zoot Suiter represents an untethered, romantic, even modernist, assertion of individuality and freedom that is far different from plebeian connection and responsibility. Like so many other popular counter-cultural identities, the ethos of the Zoot-Suit frees individuals from one mythology only to imprison them in another.

The second self is the moral self that does not just play roles but criticises them. It is experienced as the awakened conscience. It is not experienced as a second innocence, but a fallen cynicism. It gives birth to moral resolve and to ironic self-awareness simultaneously. The Zoot Suiter, on the other hand, is an exaggerated version of the first self. The young man's outlaw status is internalized and mythologized, his alienation ingested, made over, and thereby only partially conquered. By contrast, the second self of postmodern plebeian reform comes *after* heroic disillusionment. It is a form of service, not conquest. We see this lesson most clearly in the lives of Gandhi, Solzhenitsyn, and Walesa, who found their moral bearings only after rejecting petty ambition in favor of serving others in a debt of gratitude.

A Way of Response

The third lesson is that, unlike many of their contemporaries, plebeian postmoderns do not celebrate the plurality of selves or the indeterminate, modernist environment of endless change. They seek totality and organize the plurality of selves through a Self above the selves—a dialogic self, along the lines described by the literary theorist Mikhail Bakhtin, expressible only through such complex forms as the novel, the drama, or religious ritual. In other words, postmodern plebeians still honor the quest for a unifying vision capable of allowing the individual to see it all and see it whole. Such a unified and unifying perspective may be inexpressible or currently unknowable, but it is there to be realized in a novel or in a play, in a visionary appropriation of scripture, or in the transcendental deductions of nonviolent experiments in truth. This is the hope that animates their aesthetic.

Therefore postmodern plebeians do not see the psychopath as the harbinger of a new postmodern ethos. The prevailing cultural schizophrenia is something to be overcome, not capitulated to. Psychopaths represent the instability and incoherence of a society unable to initiate its citizens into the moral life of the heroic second self. Although plebeians would agree that one's ego needs to be decentered, they assume the existence of an actual divine presence ready and willing to fill the void.

In this sense, the Zoot Suiters had it half right. Any myth is better than no myth at all. But not any myth will do. There are conditioning historical circumstances to be acknowledged, thought out, discovered, defined, and then brought forward to qualify each and every affirmation. From a plebeian postmodern perspective, the best self is the second self, and the second self is the obligated self who is liberated from convention and called by destiny to help create a more inclusive community. By "destiny," I do not mean predestination or any literal divine plan *per se*. I use the term the way Martin Buber uses it, to indicate a life lived in response to the call of a higher existence, as opposed to a life of caprice based upon one's own self-defined existential projects.

In other words, in any given life or circumstance, regardless of the complexity or multiplicity of cultural meanings, there is finally one thing that must be done. What is needed is an ethic that bears down on the instant, focusing the conscience and transforming the now into the eternal. The way to the single imperative requires a willingness to hear the call of destiny in the suffering of others.

Mother Teresa answered this address when she refused to walk by one more dying man in the street. "The first one is the hardest," she has said.[9] Gandhi answered it when he refused to look away from injustice in South Africa. Walesa, when he set his people before his interests and led that first strike. Wiesel, when he vowed silence, and later again when he spoke. Solzhenitsyn, when he accepted his imprisonment as a gift from God. And Martin Luther King when he accepted the leadership of the Montgomery Improvement Association and made that first great speech at the Holt Street Church. Here the deed *is* the ethic.

Nonviolence

The fourth great lesson of plebeian postmodernism is that although politics may be the architectonic discipline, as Plato and Aristotle taught, it is *not* an autonomous science as the moderns have re-imagined it. Insofar as politics remains the art of compromise and reconciliation, the world's religious traditions still have much to teach it, especially the wisdom of nonviolence.

The Gandhian form of noncooperation with evil is, as we have seen, a recipe for cultural blending that preserves moral essences. Nonviolence rejects relativism in order to assert that only by standing in one another's essentialist shoes can we begin to understand existence from a supra-partisan perspective. Moreover, it embraces the stunning psychological paradox that the only way you can get others to stand in your shoes is to renounce any attempts to force them to do so and instead affirm your willingness to suffer out the consequences of their opposition to your values—confident that should those values prove to be less than absolute, you will be able then to adapt them in the direction of true universality. And you will be able to do so in the good conscience that no one else had to pay for your own miscalculation. This approach certifies the serious of your intentions at the same time it proves your willingness to let others have their say. And so it opens the door to dialogue at the very moment it presses forward the specific concerns of your particular cause. In other words, it asserts that solidarity, not dispassionate methodology, is the way to reconcile existential realities with essentialist moral aspirations. And the way to solidarity is to remain true to your highest ideals, even in the face of opposition, until some agreement is reached that does not do violence to what you experience as the best in yourself. The victory is not in the result, but in the deed. In fact, any attention to short term results is a form of attachment incompatible with the ultimate goal of bringing about truth and justice.

Many people forget that nonviolence is not a categorical *a priori* rejection of violence. Gandhi himself thought violence against injustice was superior to nonviolent apathy. He just thought that in the long run violence was self-defeating because it didn't create the beloved community; it merely generated new and more rigid dialectical oppositions. Violence is inherently reactionary because it imposes order; it doesn't discover it. It enforces one fictive human mythos over another; it doesn't allow for the realization of true common interests. It is not empirical, but fabulist. Nonviolence, on the other hand, is a procedure that allows us to progressively perfect our character in the confrontation with social reality. It is applicable in any and all human situations, as useful to persuading a cantankerous two-year-old to get dressed as it is in desegregating the American South.

The greatest virtue of nonviolence, however, may be the psychological change it effects upon its practitioners. Nonviolence has a power to inspire, to affirm, to enlarge one's sense of reality and of human possibility. Gandhi describes his method in terms worthy of a psychoanalyst.

> By allying myself with the weak party, by teaching him direct, firm, but harmless action, I make him feel strong and capable of defying the physical might. He feels braced for the struggle, regains confidence in himself and knowing that the remedy lies with himself, ceases to harbour the spirit of revenge and learns to be satisfied with a redress of the wrong he is seeking to remedy.[10]

In other words, nonviolence empowers individuals by enlarging their virtues and tempering their ambitions—exactly the reverse of fascism.

Nonviolence also affirms the inner life as *the* zone where political renewal takes place, and must finally be judged. And this judgment cannot simply be the glib measure of whether or not we have more money or power than in the past but must be the more profound measure of whether or not we have transcended anxiety by increasing our courage and therefore our character. In other words, nonviolence offers us an experiential measure of progress as opposed to a merely socioeconomic one and, thereby, affirms the heroics of the deep self at the very moment it decenters both the ego and the party as the origin of progressive values.

Allen Ginsberg once quipped that prayer is the highest form of epistemological research.[11] And certainly for all the religious plebeians in this book prayer is one of the keys to combating one's own stupidity and cultural trance. In its contemplative and meditative forms, prayer is more or less the art of feeling what you feel. Like nonviolence, it is instantly applicable, and so instantly enpowering, accessible to all through existential braverly. It is the art of finding that still-point within that no longer resists the pain, the emptiness, or the outrage of the moment—that simply experiences it fully and, thereby, reveals it. It is the reverse of addictions that allow one to escape feeling what one feels by altering one's consciousness. Both prayer and nonviolence demand that one accept the dark side of experience as the price one must pay to live in reality with God. One cannot simply own up to one's imperfections, one has to feel them and accept them if one is ever to free oneself from the distorting mirrors of the contending forces of history.

Once one experiences the bliss of such self-honesty, one can never know unhappiness again, at least not the kind of insatiable longing born of pursuing frantic ambitions to prove one's worth. An inner calm takes up residence at the center of one's self because one has come to love truth even more than feeling moral or being right. This alone sets us free.

Popular Need and Aristocratic Largess

There have always been two sides to the plebeian mentality: the people as oppressors and the people as liberators. Edmund Burke spells out the first side in *Reflections on the French Revolution* as do Ortega y Gasset in *Revolt of the Masses*, and Marx in his critique of the petite bourgeoisie. The second side is articulated in the great premodern mythologies of the native populations of the world, in the Old Testament prophets, the Beatitudes, the pastoral tradition, and in the Romantics. The fifth lesson is that nonviolence can reconcile aristocratic moral values with populist empiricism and practical intelligence by educating the plebeian masses to their own potential perfection. The curriculum here is not only the Arnoldian "best that has been thought and said," but the experiential curriculum of creative suffering for a just cause.

Gandhi understood that we are so afflicted by neurotic suffering these days that the real suffering of others shames us—but the sharing of that suffering cures us. Nonviolent direct action resolves the tension between modernity and tradition by connecting the individual's own personal sense of outrage and injustice to larger sublime human possibilities and, in the process, altering the individual subject's relationship to time. The Satyagrahi is not at the cutting edge of history, but neither is she or he merely waiting until the Messiah comes. He or she is living in the moment in its eternal aspect. Jacques Ellul describes this as "actualizing the eschaton"—that is to say, realizing the presence of the end in daily life. [12] For Ellul, this spiritual perspective allows the Christian to move beyond both idealism and realism to a revolutionary spirituality that is immediate, incarnational, and practical. Time ceases to be an abstraction and becomes almost a material substance that is present to hand.

In his "Letter from the Birminghham Jail" Martin Luther King spoke of the necessity to destroy the myth of time which is the notion that time itself can cure things. Time is neutral, he reminds us, to be used for good or evil. The time is always ripe to do right, but the influence of evil convinces us otherwise, teaches us to delay virtue. And this has only served to sunder us from others, from our traditions, from our best selves. Insofar as both tradition and modernity embody ideologies of time, they cannot be reconciled, but when seen from the perspective of an eschatological present they become merely two facets of the same revelation; time is material for self-creation, not a limitation.

If modernism is the recognition of the radical historicity of perception and meaning, then plebeian postmodernism is this same recognition after history itself has been seen through as a power play. And so the postmodern plebeian examines events with an eye to their meaning as remembrance and response to the original sacred blessing of the earth in Creation. The so-called end of philosophy may merely be one more apocalyptic mystification obscuring the need to reflect on the origins and destiny of humanity in the concrete terms of immediate moral obligation.

Another way of stating this distinction is that modernists see history as a nightmare from which they are trying to awaken, while postmodernists believe it is vain to try to wake up to any pristine reality free from mythic overlay. A better approach is to gain control over this nightmare through the strategies of lucid dreaming. One can learn to recognize the phantasmagoric nature of reality itself (this is the poet's secret) and so ease history into new directions by entering into its evolving patterns and altering its metaphoric self-descriptions, not by searching for some Archimedean point of absolute truth in things or words or ontological structures.

Again it might seem that there is not really too great a difference here between the postmodern plebeian's strategies for reform and Pound's modernist literary project to "make it new." But what is different is the sense in which one makes it new. Not by revolutionizing consciousness, inventing whole new aesthetics and universes of discourse, but by bearing in on the existential moment, however oddly it may be described or understood, and eternalizing it much in the way Mother Teresa eternalizes the suffering of the man dying in the street: by seeing it as the actual suffering of God.

In this context our everyday problems become the contours of our destiny and by extension the very image of the age within which we live. Here the high modern insight that ontology is historically defined, and that we make ourselves by remaking the structures that make us, ceases to be a justification for the existential projects of Supermarket Supermen, but instead becomes an abiding and humbling recognition of one's obligations to the past and to others as constitutive of who we are.

The plebeian move is into history, not epistemology. The modernist avant-garde, instead of rejecting the Cartesian dualism of mind and matter, moved more deeply into its dilemmas, seeking the premise behind the premise in ever more refined analyses of the categories of thought. Plebeian postmoderns, however, prefer to historicize and moralize perception. They turn perception into an adventure in meaning, a creative practical act that cannot be separated out into any autonomous realm independent of one's responsibility to other persons as persons. This synthesis of knowing with doing, so central to the doctrine of nonviolence, reconciles popular need with aristocratic largesse.

Literariness and the Plebeian Sublime

The sixth key lesson of plebeian postmodernism is that the postmodern notion of literariness offers us a way to transform classical religious dogmas into transparent spiritual mythologies, rendering them open to dialogue with other traditions. I am referring primarily to the work of Jakobson, Mukarovsky, and Barthes, all of whom see literature as discourse that is freed from the constraints of literal reference but still capable of putting meaning into the world. Roland Barthes defined literariness this way:

How can a text, which consists of language, be outside languages. How exteriorize the world's jargons without taking refuge in an ultimate jargon wherein the others would simply be reported, cited? As soon as I name, I am named: caught in the rivalry of names. How can the text "get itself out" of the war of fictions, of sociolects?—by a gradual labor of extenuation. First the text liquidates all metalanguage, whereby it is text: no voice (Science, Cause, Institution) is behind what it is saying. Next, the text destroys utterly to the point of contradiction, its own discursive category, its sociolinguistic reference (its "genre"): it is the comical that does not make us laugh, the irony which does not subjugate, the jubilation without soul, without mystique (Sarduy), quotation without quotation marks. Lastly, the text can, if it wants, attack the canonical structures of language itself. . . It is a matter of effecting, by transmutation (and no longer by transformation) a new philosophical state of the language-substance.[13]

Literariness, in this sense, is a form of rhetorical nonviolence. It refuses to take up the arms of definition; instead it tries to generate a new level of communication and communion from within the already understood, but unspoken and perhaps previously unspeakable realms of shared human experience.

This recognition of the value of literary discourse as potentially more complex, theoretically self-aware and practically applicable than so-called literal language serves to expose the descriptive jargons of the social sciences as pietist attempts to speak from a position of universal history that simply does not and cannot exist. Literature, the language of scripture, poetry, ritual, and other "lovers' discourses" are more productive avenues for transcending the ideological, for they need not be logically clarified to become epistemologically valid; their meanings are experiential and apodictic. Hence the old traditions, read through the postmodern lens of literariness, cease being dogmatic and become spiritual again as expressions of the sublime. Such a reading allows us to connect with the past and transcend it at the same time.

Bernard-Henri Levy described this postmodern religiosity this way:

Monotheism . . . is neither a monism nor a theism, but a concrete ethics, a celebration of Law, a pledge on the Universal, and a miracle of Reason, whose impossible figure is perhaps the surest and last recourse against the dangers of voluntary surrender and submission . . . the morality of resistance, the systematic anti-fascism which this century has forced us to adopt, may find its only chance to take on reality in the memory of the One God and His passion for the law.[14]

The idea here that systematic antifascism can become *real* only through God and Law is not a defense of existing institutions or a reactionary return to theocracy. It is, rather, an acknowledgment that the masters of modernity may have misread essentialist philosophies altogether, as did the dogmatic premodern adherents of such systems. There need be nothing absolute about religious absolutes except in the mind that idolizes them and transforms them from a grand trope into a normative metaphysic.

For postmodern plebeians the traditional faiths had it half right. God exists, but it is not so easy to know that. We must earn our spiritual understanding through acts of bravery and trust; only then will faith and knowledge follow as a gift. We cannot will spiritual insight or assume we ever completely possess it. The quest for a meta-theory makes no sense if one is looking for the sign behind the sign that grounds all knowing in some indisputable absolute. But it can make sense as a novelistic conceit posited to elaborate on what we already know so that we can act on it. That is to say, we can still think cosmologically if we speak metaphorically, but if we speak positively we can only think methodologically. And so the quest for the literal dooms us to idioms of increasing abstraction and self-reference, sundered forever from the moral imperative to act and connect with others. Literariness and the traditions of the sublime free us from such conundrums and offer the postmodern plebeian both a way to connect with the past and to transcend it. The postmodern plebeian has, in Sanford Krolick's phrase, a "recollective resolve, a personal authenticity constituted by his or her being-toward-the-beginning."[15] The present moment of existence and the possibilities of the future are empowered by a fundamentally constitutive past. In common language, this means that ordinary people find themselves bound by particular cultural contexts, yet these very determinations become sources of power once they are seen as invitations to transcendence.

The Problematics of Assimilation

The seventh lesson is that the theme of alienation, which presumed a deep Romantic self torn from its moorings, has given way to the problematics of assimilation. Unlike the assimilated middle class, economically excluded peoples such as the Polish workers or Native Americans have enduring memories as a people impressed forever in their rituals, customs, and myths. These traditions represent counter-aesthetics that preserve a sense of self quite different from the sense of self found in the postindustrial world. Third-world and ethnic literatures are instructive in many ways, but above all they tell the tale of the confrontation of entire cultures with the modern, not merely the individual emigre's predictably alienated response to the obsolescence of his or her traditions. Such literature more directly considers the questions of assimilation, of what is best in a people, what is best given up, and how one is to live with the death of one's gods—or at least their displacement.

In their preface to *The Symposium of the Whole* (1983), Jerome and Diane Rothenberg explain this relationship between modernity and plebeianism in slightly different terms.

> When the industrial West began to discover—and plunder— "new" and "old" worlds beyond its boundaries, an extraordinary countermovement came into being in the West itself. Alongside the official ideologies that shoved European man to the apex of the human pyramid, there were some thinkers and artists who found ways of doing and knowing among other peoples as complex as any European and often virtually erased from European consciousness. Cultures described as "primitive" and "savage"—as a stage below barbarian were simultaneously the models for political and social experiments, religious and visionary revivals, and forms of art and poetry so different from European norms as to be revolutionary from a later Western perspective.
>
> It was almost, looking back at it, as if every radical innovation in the West were revealing a counterpart—or series of counterparts somewhere in the traditional worlds the West was savaging.[16]

Although the emphasis here is on establishing the relevance of ethno-poetics to our postmodern era, the Rothenbergs nevertheless provide us with a vision of the plebeian as home-grown primitive. The very trait that made indigenous people so powerful as cultural entities—their total lack of theoretical self-consciousness in living out their sacred mythologies—was turned by the modern world into a psychological vice, political weakness, and logical fallacy. Since the Enlightenment, theoretical self-consciousness has become the measure of epistemological validity and mathematics the paradigm of all real knowledge. Sciences gained epistemological prestige exactly to the degree to which they could incorporate mathematical models into their own inquiries.

It has taken the indigenous people of the world several centuries to respond to this challenge, but their defenses, and with them all the defenses of the preindustrial modes of thinking and perception from Blake to Joseph Campbell, redefine the cultural dynamics of our present age. Unconscious capacity, intuitive connection, tacit knowing, psychological density are all finding their value again. Reflection and critique are not seen as ends in themselves but as ways to integrate knowledge. And alienation, once seen as the measure of one's cultural liberation, is now only one phase in the psychological voyage of postmodern plebeians.

It has become increasingly apparent that inside every class within every nation there is an indigenous, plebeian underground, a wellspring of resistance to the dehumanizing aspects of modernization. Something in the plebeians' backgrounds, be they Third or First World, thwarts their capacity to find a comfortable place within the modern world. Perhaps they are too religious, too conservative, too sensitive, too Black, too poor, too female, too gay, too Romantic, or too beat to become fully conscious of what is in their own self-interest in materialist terms. In self-defense, the "new" plebeians mount their own historical critiques of the status quo. This new self-consciousness changes their status from alienated outsiders doomed to "ignorant perfection" to rebels engaged with the problematics of assimilation, seeking reform in ways that are unintelligible to their oppressors or, for that matter, to their more assimilated peers, who have unconsciously adapted to the new socio-economic order with little sense that anything has been lost or compromised.

The lives of such plebeians thus mirror the dilemmas of the age. How does one carry one's culture, heritage, and conscience into the future without betraying those who came before? How does one survive without giving up the rich complexity that constitutes one's inner life with all its gratuitous commitments and obligations?

Conclusion: Redeeming Practical Reason

In the postmodern plebeian sensibility the two great strands of modern European philosophy meet: the systems of Hegel, Marx, and the later Sartre, and the existentialisms of Kierkegaard, Nietzsche, and Camus. The systems provide the intellectual contexts, the terms, the principal post-Enlightenment categories; the existentialisms express the survival of a fugitive humanism, an underground personalism (i.e., what is left of traditional ethics).

Plebeian postmoderns identify with the goals and premises of the existential tradition. For them "the end of history is the victory of existential time over historical time, of creative subjectivity over objectivization, of personality over the universal common, of existential society over objectivized society."[17] But they *think* dialectically. That is to say, their thought attempts to integrate their antagonists into a larger framework and to refuse the bad faith of pretending their own perspectives are free from bias or outside the processes of history. They seek a pluralistic worldview capable of preserving the integrity of indigenous mythologies and preindustrial values without giving up the Western philosophical quest for absolutes. This reconciliation of essentialist and existentialist perspectives cannot be accomplished within the old reductive, materialist methodologies or within the assumptions of monist idealistic philosophies; it requires a new historicism, a new sense of the radical contextuality of values and their instrumental nature as the tools of practical reason.

But even were we to articulate such a postmodern worldview, it would not be enough to bring about enlighted change because the vices of the people—mediocrity, sentimentality, ethnocentrism, and superstition—are not the products of philosophical misunderstanding *per se* but of a stunted imagination and a misapplied will. The perfection of practical reason, therefore, cannot proceed merely along the lines of a pure Kantian transcendental reflection but must somehow incorporate a grasp of particulars, exceptions, irreducible individualities, and one-of-a-kind creative opportunities. Practical reason must be embodied in leadership, and it must somehow appropriate the ancient arts of discernment that were aimed at educating the imagination to the actual possibilities inherent in the implied order of the whole.

In other words, practical reason, which Kant described as "everything which is possible by or through freedom,"[18] has to discover its limits and direction before it can perfect its aims. The spiritual disciplines of prayer, fasting, and meditation (not to mention their literary counterparts in the arts of self-irony and metaphoric redescription) were designed to do just that—temper the will to a realistic appraisal of its place within the whole so that when we do act, or reflect, or speak out, we do so in harmony with the entire trajectory of creative existence as revealed by the founding mythos of our own cultures of origin. Each particular practice may require its own particular set of virtues, but the ends of each particular art are themselves determined by imperatives built into the visionary impulses of the culture at large.

There need be no magic or supernaturalism involved here; the arts of discernment are disciplines of self-limitation. They test limits and create leaders—prayer through an acute listening to the implications of our deepest hopes, fears, and expectations; fasting by measuring the degree of our commitments, nonviolence through wholehearted confrontation with our enemies; and meditation by revealing the mind's own processes, cover-ups, subterfuges and bad faith. Such revelations alter how we understand the meaning of our projects and ideas. Thus they serve to curb prejudice, sentimentality, superstition, and ethnocentrism by constantly putting our particular existential projects into contact with a larger, humbling, previously unimagined conception of the whole.

Also, unlike their modernist precursors, plebeian postmoderns do not attempt to overcome the traditional plebeian vices through a direct assault upon their metaphysical premises. Rather they seek to limit their excesses by perfecting plebeian practical reason and thus altering how those metaphysical assumptions are understood. Their's is not a search for a method or even for a ground upon which to build a new phenomenology or philosophical anthropology, so much as a quest for consistency—for integrity and accuracy within the givens of one's own particular cultural-historical matrix.

Put simply, postmodern plebeian leaders reread the imperatives of the sacred traditions in more psychologically and politically circumspect environments than did their ancestors, thereby altering the meanings of those traditions to our time without cancelling their claim to timelessness. Gandhi, for example, did not invent the fast, nor did he alter any of the essential tenets of Hinduism. His innovation was to apply them to the problems of modern public life with a consistency and perfection hitherto unimagined. The same may be said of Mother Teresa's Catholicism, Martin Luther King's Protestantism, and Wiesel's Judaism. All of them were experimenting with the creative truth of their own cultures of origin, testing it through application against the circumstances of their times. They moved toward a transcendental reflection upon the holistic significance of particular actions, using mythic, as opposed to rational, categories of understanding. Then they worked outward again toward a practical application of that wisdom.

For them, resanctifying life is a goal, not a starting point. So one cannot derive a theology or metaphysic directly from any authority; one has to discover its operation in practice. This transformation of premise into goal has the effect of cancelling sentimentality, parochialism, and moral rigidity by exposing their origins in the totalitarian impulses for system and order, not in the radically free moment of choice. Thus plebeian postmodernism defines an ethic capable of replacing both the moral ambivalence of the existing order and the reductionist counter-theses of the new barbarisms. Plebeian postmodernism is, however, no simple pastoralism. It is a critique of the people by the people themselves that articulates their weaknesses as well as celebrating their strengths.

Yet like the pastoral the new plebeianism contrasts these ethical strengths and weaknesses against the world at large in order to dramatize certain irreconcilable differences between the people and their circumstances. Whereas the traditional pastoral celebrated the old aristocratic virtues by showing us rustics who unconsciously embodied them, the new plebeians contrast the morality of the excluded against the privileges of the powerful in order both to criticize society and to initiate the people into the voyage toward the second self.

The "people," often dubbed the "carriers of history," have in reality been mostly absent from it. As Marx argued, their moral criticism has been impotent. Their historic role has been to stand in the way of their own deliverance. The big lie has been that the middle-class plebeian rules contemporary culture, when in fact, middle-class individuals are engaged in a hopeless search for essential life in a society devoid of ultimate concerns. Economics rules, and even in the advanced countries middle-class plebeians do not live easily with this truth. Like their Romantic precursors before them, they are trying to preserve a sense of the deeper life in a hostile environment.

Ironically, this very longing for a more profound existence makes them prey to salesmen and commercial visionaries who sell them dreams without inspiring them to the discipline necessary for authentic transcendence. They become consumers—systematically miseducated, underestimated, financially pampered, and morally exploited. They are nonpersons who are celebrated by the media as existentially free but whose history, ethnicity, personality, and moral seriousness have been marginalized, if not entirely debunked, by a world socioeconomic order that runs according to its own impersonal rules and agenda.

Nonetheless, a religious plebeian leadership has emerged with antidotes to these developments; calling for a new elevated sense of the self as socially and historically constituated and therefore inherently politically engaged and morally responsible.

In his book, *Reaching Out* (1975), Henri Nouwen remarks:

> We cannot change the world by a new plan, project, or idea. We cannot even change other people by our convictions, stories, advice and proposals, but we can offer a space where people are encouraged to disarm themselves, lay aside their occupations and preoccupations and listen with attention and care to the voices speaking in their own center.[19]

Offering that space is the task of a plebeian postmodern culture. Is it surprising that the voices emerging are those of our ancestral forebears, and that the words they speak come from our most compassionate spiritual traditions? Is it surprising that the deeds of our postmodern saints register as an ironic challenge against the antihumanism of the most advanced theoretical thought of our age?

There is, indeed, a light in this world—a healing spirit more powerful than any darkness we may encounter. "We sometimes lose sight of this force when there is suffering—too much pain. And suddenly this spirit emerges through the lives of ordinary people who hear a call and respond in extraordinary ways."[20] In our time these different individuals collect to form a shared witness to the importance of the individual person and to the lost sublimity of our traditions.

We are, it seems, exquisite creatures of the sublime—born to novelty, invention, challenge, and transcendence. How long can we simply repeat the revolutions of the last two centuries? We are called beyond such ordinary business to a perfection that is no longer ignorant.

NOTES

Introduction

1. Dietrich Bonhoeffer, *Letters and Papers from Prison*, ed. Eberhard Bethge (New York: Macmillan, 1972), 16–17; reprint, originally 1953.

2. Judy Grahn, for instance, in *Another Mother Tongue* (Boston: Beacon Press, 1984) seeks to define the original lesbian culture in the West, and Carol Padden and Tom Humphries attempt to define an original culture for the deaf in their book *Deaf in America* (Boston: Harvard University Press, 1988). There are any number of other examples of this attempt to recover one's founding mythology, from the vision of Atzlan that inspired the Chicano literary renaissance of the nineteen sixties to the revisionist histories being born inside Poland's Solidarity Movement.

3. Gustavo Gutierrez, *The Power of the Poor in History*, trans. Robert R. Barr (Maryknoll, NY: Orbis Press, 1983), 191.

4. Henri Nouwen, *Reaching Out* (New York: Walker, 1985), 135; reprint, originally 1975.

Chapter One. Ignorant Perfection

1. Robert Bly, "A Few Notes on Antonio Machado," in *Times Alone: Selected Poems of Antonio Machado*, chosen and trans. by Robert Bly (Middletown, CT: Wesleyan University Press, 1983), 14.

2. Georg Lukács, *Solzhenitsyn*, trans. William David Graf (Cambridge, MA: MIT Press, 1970), 64–65.

3. For an extended discussion of the differences between Lukácsian neo-Marxism and Solzhenitsyn's plebeianism, see Irving Howe, "The Straight and the Crooked: Solzhenitsyn and Lukacs," *The Critical Point* (New York: Horizon Press, 1973), 93.

4. Karl Marx, *The Eighteenth Brumaire of Louis Bonaparte* (New York: International, 1963), 15; reprint, originally 1852.

5. Perhaps the two classics in this genre are Czeslaw Milosz's *Captive Mind* (New York: Random House, 1981) and Milovan Djilas's *New Class* (San Diego: Harcourt Brace Jovanovich, 1982).

6. George Santayana, "A General Confession," *The Philosophy of George Santayana*, 2d ed., ed. Paul A. Schilpp (New York: Tudor Press, 1951), 17.

7. I am thinking here of books like Anthony Wilden's *System and Structure* (London: Tavistok, 1972), Theodore Adorno's *Negative Dialectics* (New York: Seabury, 1973), and Jean-Paul Sartre's *Critique of Dialectical Reason*, ed. Alan Sheridan (New York: Routledge, Chapman, & Hall, 1976).

8. The postmodern plebeian has, in Sanford Krolick's phrase, a "recollective resolve," a personal authenticity constituted by his or her "being-toward-the-beginning." The present moment of existence and the possibilities of the future are empowered by a fundamentally constitutive past. See Sanford Krolick, *Recollective Resolve: A Phenomenological Understanding of Time and Myth* (Macon, Ga.: Mercer University Press, 1987).

This view, confirmed by contemporary biochemist and cell biologist Rupert Sheldrake, acknowledges that all natural systems inherit a collective memory of their kind encoded in their very structure ("formative causation"). This includes crystals, mammals, insects, and human beings. The laws of nature are like habits—not mathematical inevitabilities—and so the universe itself is literally an historical entity, not a material mass. Its physical make-up is a repository of past deeds, acts, and choices—each past system remaining present in a "morphic field" that is more or less a collective memory that transcends time-space conditions. In human societies history lives as much in the individual's instinct for freedom and urge for meaning as it does in institutions. The past and the present are mutually evoked in the existential anxieties of the individual. And should the record of civilization be destroyed, humanity could, as Carl Jung once observed, recreate it out of its own dream life or, perhaps more radically, out of the inherent originality of its own morphic field.

See Rupert Sheldrake, *The Presence of the Past* (New York: Random House, 1989), and David Ray Griffin's essay "Bohm and Whitehead on Wholeness, Freedom, Causality, and Time," in David Ray Griffin ed., *Physics and the Ultimate Significance of Time* (Albany, NY: State University of New York Press, 1986), 127.

9. The phrase comes from Lech Walesa's autobiography, *A Way of Hope* (New York: Henry Holt, 1987).

10. This phrase comes from Norman Mailer's essay on totalitarianism in *The Idol and the Octopus* (New York: Dell, 1968), 122.

11. For an analysis of the way capital works to collapse space-time distinctions and remap the metaphysical universe, see David Harvey, *The Condition of Postmodernity* (Cambridge, MA.: Basil Blackwell, 1989).

Chapter Two. Gandhi

1. Fyodor Dostoevsky, *The Brothers Karamazov*, trans. Constance Garnett (New York: Random House, 1950), 65.

2. Martin Buber, *Pointing the Way*, trans. and ed. Maurice Friedman (New York: Harper & Row, 1957), 126.

3. See Mahatma Gandhi, "Neither Saint Nor Politician" in *The Collected Works of Mahatma Gandhi*, XVII, February–June 1920 (Ahmedabad, India: Ministry of Information & Broadcasting, Government of India), 406. Also quoted in Buber, *Pointing the Way*, 128.

4. Buber, *Pointing the Way*, 129.

5. Coretta Scott King, ed., *The Words of Martin Luther King* (New York: Newmarket Press, 1984), 74.

6. George Orwell, "Reflections on Gandhi," *A Collection of Essays by George Orwell* (Garden City, NY: Doubleday, 1954), 183.

7. *Gandhi* a film directed and produced by Richard Attenborough.

8. Krishna Kripalani, ed., *All Men Are Brothers* (Ahmedabad, India: Navajivan, 1960), 83.

9. See Frederick Douglass, *Life and Times of Frederick Douglass* (New York: Collier, 1962), originally published 1892.

10. William Borman, *Gandhi and Non-Violence* (Albany, NY: State University of New York Press, 1986).

11. Borman, *Gandhi and Non-Violence*, 200.

12. Paul Ricoeur, *The Symbolism of Evil* (Boston: Beacon Press, 1967), 355.

13. Ricoeur, *The Symbolism of Evil*, 356.

14. Kripalani, *All Men Are Brothers*, 178.

15. Milan Kundera, "Esch is Luther," trans. David Rieff, published as the Afterword to *Terra Nostra* by Carlos Fuentes, trans. Margaret Sayers Peden (New York: Farrar, Straus & Giroux, 1987), 786; originally published 1976.

16. Martin Green, *The Challenge of the Mahatmas* (New York: Basic Books, 1978), 152.

17. Green, *The Challenge of the Mahatmas*, 162.

18. Martin Green, *The Origins of Nonviolence* (University Park, PA: Pennsylvania State University Press, 1986).

19. Louis Fischer ed., *The Essential Gandhi* (New York: Random House, 1983), 320; originally published 1962.

20. The complete quote is "Look, I can see you don't play any instruments. Whatever are you talking about? In the house there are all your worries. The wife. The children. What are we going to eat? How shall we manage for clothes? What will become of us? Hell! No, for the santuri you must be in good form, you must be pure. If my wife says one word too many, how could I possibly be in the mood to play the santuri? If your children are hungry and screaming at you, you just try to play! To play the santuri you have to give everything up to it, d'you understand?" Nikos Kazantzakis, *Zorba the Greek*, trans. Carl Wildman (New York: Simon & Schuster, 1952), 13.

21. Carl Jung, *Psychology and Religion: West and East*, trans. R. F. C. Hull, vol. 2 of the *Collected Works*, Bollinger Series, no. 20, 2d. edition (Princeton, NJ: Princeton University Press, 1973), 75.

22. Eknath Easwaran, *Gandhi the Man* (Petaluma CA: Nilgiri Press, 1978), 170–171; originally published 1972.

Chapter Three. Solzhenitsyn

1. Gutierrez, *The Power of the Poor*, 230.

2. See Hans Gadamer, "Hermeneutics of Suspicion," in *Hermeneutics: Questions and Prospects*, ed. Gary Shapiro and Alan Sica (Amherst, MA: University of Massachusetts Press, 1982), 54.

3. This phrase comes from Richard Falk's description of the ethical imperatives of the emerging postmodern ethic. See Richard Falk, "In Pursuit of the Postmodern," *Spirituality and Society* ed. David Ray Griffin (Albany, NY: State University of New York Press, 1988).

4. Solzhenitsyn, "Address to the Nobel Festival," in *Solzhenitsyn: A Documentary Record*, 2d ed., ed. Leopold Labedz (New York: Harper & Row, 1972), 252–53.

5. I heard these remarks at the Modern Language Association convention in Washington, D.C., December 28, 1984, at the panel on "Morality and Literature," a program arranged by the Association of Departments of English.

6. Solzhenitsyn, *The Oak and the Calf*, trans. Harry Willets (New York: Harper & Row, 1980), 307.

7. Solzhenitsyn, *Gulag Archipelago: An Experiment in Literary Investigation I–II*, trans. by Thomas P. Whitney (New York: Harper & Row, l973), 591.

8. Solzhenitsyn, *Gulag Archipelago*, 591.

9. Solzhenitsyn, *Gulag Archipelago*, 592.

10. The complete reference from Foucault reads as follows (from *Power/Knowledge*, ed. Colin Gordon [New York: Pantheon Books, 1980], 137–38):

No doubt it would be a mistake to conceive the plebs as the permanent ground of history, the final objective of all subjections, the ever smouldering center of all revolts. The plebs is [sic] no doubt a real sociological entity. But there is indeed always something in the social body, in classes, groups, and individuals themselves which in some sense escapes relations of power, something which is by no means a more or less docile or reactive primal matter, but rather a centrifugal movement, an inverse energy, a discharge. There is certainly no such thing as 'the' plebs; rather there is, as it were, a certain plebeian quality or aspect ('de la' plebe). There is plebs in bodies, in souls, in the individual, in the proletariat, in the bourgeoisie, but everywhere in a diversity of forms and extensions, of energies and irreducibilities. . . This point of view of the plebs, the point of view of the underside and limit of power, is thus indispensable for an analysis of its apparatuses (dispositifs); this is the starting point for understanding its functioning and developments. I don't think this can be confused in any way with a neo-populism that substantializes the plebs as an entity, or a neo-liberalism that sanctifies its basic rights.

11. Gary Snyder, *The Old Ways* (San Francisco: City Lights, 1977), 37.

12. Solzhenitsyn, *The Oak and the Calf*, 7–8.

13. "An Interview with Aleksandr Solzhenitsyn," by Janis Sapiets in Solzhenitsyn, *East and West* (New York: Perennial Library, 1980), 158–160.

14. Solzhenitsyn, *Gulag Archipelago III–IV* (New York: Harper & Row, 1975), 610.

Chapter Four. Wiesel

1. Carol Rittner, "An Interview with Elie Wiesel," *America* 159, no. 15 (Nov. 19, 1988): 400.

2. See Michael Walzer, *Exodus and Revolution* (New York: Basic Books, 1985), and Desmond Tutu's essay "Liberation as a Biblical Theme" in *Hope and Suffering* compiled by Mothobi Mutloatse, ed. John Webster (Grand Rapids, MI: Eerdmans, 1984), 48–87.

3. Elie Wiesel, *The Town Beyond the Wall* (New York: Avon, 1969), 190; originally published 1964.

4. Elie Wiesel, *Twilight*, trans. Marion Wiesel (New York: Summit Books, 1988), 209.

5. Elie Wiesel, *The Night Trilogy* (New York: Hill & Wang, 1987), 72; originally published 1960.

6. *Responses to Elie Wiesel*, ed. Harry James Cargas, (New York: Persea Books, 1978), 10, 13, quoted in Robert McAfee Brown, *Elie Wiesel: Messenger to All Humanity* (Notre Dame, IN: University of Notre Dame Press, 1983), 40.

7. Brown, *Elie Wiesel*, 44.

8. Elie Wiesel, *Zalmen, or the Madness of God* (New York: Random House, 1974), 79.

9. Elie Wiesel, *To Be a Jew* (New York: Vintage Books, 1978), 9–10.

10. Elie Wiesel, *Somewhere a Master: Further Hasidic Portraits and Legends* (New York: Summit Books, 1982), 12.

11. Wiesel, *To Be a Jew*, 8.

12. Wiesel, *The Night Triology*, 135.

13. Elie Wiesel, *Beggar in Jerusalem*, trans. Lily Edelman and the author (New York: Random House, 1970), 113.

Chapter Five. Mother Teresa

1. Gutierrez, *The Power of the Poor*, 200.

2. Malcolm Muggeridge, *Something Beautiful for God* (San Francisco: Harper & Row, 1971), 127.

3. Muggeridge, *Something Beautiful for God*, 112–113.

4. Muggeridge, *Something Beautiful for God*, 22.

5. Muggeridge, *Something Beautiful for God*, 5.

6. Muggeridge, *Something Beautiful for God*, 30.

7. Mother Teresa, *A Gift for God*, ed. Malcolm Muggeridge (San Francisco: Harper & Row, 1975), 3.

8. Mother Teresa, *A Gift for God*, 70.

9. Mother Teresa, *A Gift for God*, 21.

10. Robert Bly, "Men and the Wound," keynote address, Midwest Regional Men's Conference, Minneapolis, Minnesota, October 12, 1985.

11. Thomas Merton, *Thoughts in Solitude* (New York: Farrar, Straus & Giroux, 1976), 18, 20.

12. Jerome Klinkowitz, *Rosenberg/Barthes/Hassan: The Postmodern Habit of Thought* (Athens, GA: University of Georgia Press, 1988), 23.

13. Harold Rosenberg, *Artworks and Packages* (New York: Horizon, 1969), 226.

14. I am using Thomas Merton's definition of symbolism here. See Thomas Merton, "Symbolism: Communication or Communion" in

Love and Living, ed. Naomi Burton Stone and Brother Patrick Hart (New York: Farrar, Straus & Giroux, 1979), 59.

15. Herman Hesse, *Magister Ludi* (New York: Holt, Rinehart & Winston, 1969), 67.

16. Kathryn Spink, ed., *Life in the Spirit* (San Francisco: Harper & Row, 1983), 75.

17. Jerry Brown, "A Passage to India: Working with Mother Teresa," *Life* (April, 1988): 28–32.

18. Brown, "A Passage to India," 32.

19. Spink, *Life in the Spirit,* 72–73.

Chapter Six. Martin Luther King

1. Reinhold Niebuhr, *The Nature and Destiny of Man,* vol. 2 (New York: Charles Scribner's Sons, 1945), 285–86; reprint, originally 1943.

2. Quoted in Harold Bloom, *Ruin the Sacred Truths* (Cambridge, MA: Harvard University Press, 1989), 117.

3. Bloom, *Ruin the Sacred Truths,* 5.

4. Vincent Harding, "Getting Ready for the Hero," *Sojourners* 15, no. 1 (Jan. 1986): 18.

5. See Taylor Branch, *Parting the Waters* (New York: Simon & Schuster, 1988). This narrative biographical history of the civil rights movement in the United States uses the polyvalent strategies of Solzhenitsyn's own experiments in literary history—shifting points of view depending upon the particular individual being examined. In revealing the character of Martin Luther King, he often shifts from King's views of Kennedy, Hoover, Malcolm X, and Niebuhr to their views of him—all rendered in their historical context and given significance through the unfolding historical conflicts.

6. Branch, *Parting the Waters,* 217.

7. "Superman Comes to the Supermarket" first appeared in *Esquire Magazine,* March, 1963, and was reprinted in Norman Mailer, *The Idol and the Octopus* (New York: Dell, 1968), 30.

8. Christopher Lasch, *The Minimal Self* (New York: Norton, 1984), 258.

9. Martin Luther King, Jr., *Strength to Love* (Philadelphia: Fortress Press, 1986) 118; reprint, originally 1977.

10. James M. Washington, ed., *Testament of Hope* (San Francisco: Harper & Row, 1986), 347.

11. For the connection of this phrase with liberation theology, see Dennis P. McCann, *Christian Realism and Liberation Theology* (Maryknoll, NY: Orbis Books, 1982).

12. Bill Kellermann, "Apologist of Power," *Sojourners* 16, no. 3, (March 1987): 14.

13. Branch, *Parting the Waters*, 702.

14. John Lavey, "Personalism," *The Enclycopedia of Philosophy* vol. 6, ed. Paul Edwards (New York: Macmillan, 1972), 109.

15. King, *Strength to Love*, 147–155.

16. Coretta King, *Words of Martin Luther King*, 47.

17. Adam Michnik, "Why You Are Not Signing . . . A Letter From Bialoeka Internment Camp 1982," *Letters from Prison*, trans. Maya Latynski (Berkeley, Ca: University of California Press, 1985), 88–89.

18. King, *Strength to Love*, 118.

19. John J. Ansbro, *Martin Luther King Jr.: The Making of a Mind* (Maryknoll, NY: Orbis Books, 1982), 140.

20. King, *Strength to Love*, 120.

21. Robert Coles, "On the Nature of Character," *Daedalus* 110, no. 4 (Fall, 1981); reprinted in Wayne C. Booth and Marshall W. Gregory eds., *The Harper & Row Reader* (New York: Harper & Row, 1984), 281.

22. King, *Strength to Love*, 124.

23. King, *Strength to Love*, 126.

24. James H. Cone, "A Dream or a Nightmare," in *Sojourners* 15, no. 1 (January 1986): 30.

25. Cone, "A Dream or a Nightmare," 30.

26. King, *Strength to Love*, 124.

27. King, *Strength to Love*, 134.

28. King, *Strength to Love*, 90.

29. Branch, *Parting the Waters*, 140–41.

Chapter Seven. Walesa

1. Antonio Gramsci, "The Mode of Existence of the New Intellectual," *The Modern Prince and Other Writings* (London: Lawrence & Wishat, 1957), 122.

2. Gramsci, "The Mode of Existence," 118.

3. Gramsci, "The Mode of Existence," 122.

4. Gramsci, "The Mode of Existence," 79–80.

5. Gramsci, "The Mode of Existence," 81.

6. See John Hellman, "The Prophets of Solidarity," in *America* 147 (Nov. 6, 1982): 266.

7. Maria Janion, "On the Difference Between a 'Worker' and a 'Representative of the Working Class' trans. Boleslaw Taborsici in ed. Edmund Szczcsiak et al., *The Book of Lech Walesa* (New York: Simon & Schuster, 1982), 128.

8. Andrzej Drzycimski, "Growing," trans. Celina Wieniewska in *The Book of Lech Walesa*, 73.

9. Roman Wapinski, "On Mass Movements and Their Leaders," trans. Boleslaw Taborski in *The Book of Lech Walesa*, 128.

10. Lech Walesa, *A Way of Hope*, trans. Marek B. Zaleski et al. (New York: Henry Holt & Co., 1987), 288.

11. Janion, "On the Difference," 126.

12. Walesa, *A Way of Hope*, 121–122.

13. "I Am Always Free," interview with Lech Walesa, *Reader's Digest* 124 (May, 1984): 108.

14. "I Am Always Free," 108.

15. Walesa, *A Way of Hope*, 145.

16. Walesa, *A Way of Hope*, 163–64.

17. John Tagliabue, "Lech! Lech!" New York Times Sunday Magazine (October 23, 1988): 42.

18. Jonathan Schell, "A Better Today," *The New Yorker* (March 25, 1985): 35.

19. Quoted in Drzycimski, "Growing," 103.

20. Gramsci, "The Mode of Existence," 79–80.

21. Walesa, *A Way of Hope*, 3–4.

22. "I Am Always Free," 110.

23. Alexander Solzhenitsyn, "A World Split Apart," in *Vital Speeches of the Day* 44, no. 22 (September 1, 1978): 681.

Chapter Eight. The Modernization of Poverty, Stupidity, and Family Life

1. Emmanuel Mounier, *Personalism*, quoted in frontspiece to Stephen Frederick Schneck, *Persons and Polis: Max Scheler's Personalism as Political Theory* (Albany, NY: State University of New York Press, 1987).

2. For a collection of essays setting forth Illich's views on the whole range of the disutilities of modernism, see Ivan Illich, *Towards a History of Needs* (New York: Bantam, 1980) and *Celebration of Awareness* (Garden City, NY: Doubleday, 1970).

3. Ivan Illich, "Energy and Equity," *Towards a History of Needs*, 144.

4. Alberto Moravia, *The Red Book and the Great Wall*, trans. Ronald Strom (New York: Farrar, Straus & Giroux, 1968), 7–8.

5. *Mother Teresa*, a film produced and directed by Ann Petrie and Jeanette Petrie.

6. Milan Kundera, "Jersusalem Address: The Novel and Europe," *The Art of the Novel* (New York: Grove Press, 1988), 162–163.

7. Dietrich Bonhoeffer, "After Ten Years," in *Letters & Papers from Prison*, ed. Eberhard Bethge (New York: Macmillan, 1972) 8–9.

8. Solzhenitsyn, *The Oak and the Calf*, 247.

9. Bonhoeffer, "After Ten Years," 9.

10. Mother Teresa, *A Gift for God*, 12–13.

11. R. D. Laing, *The Politics of Experience* (New York: Ballantine, 1967), 65.

12. Sinclair Lewis, *Babbit* (New York: Signet, 1961), 85; originally published 1922.

13. Antonio Machado, *Times Alone*, ed. and trans. Robert Bly (Middletown, CT: Wesleyan University Press, 1983), 53.

14. Roberty Bly, "Five Stages in Exiling, Hunting, and Retrieving the Shadow," in William Booth, ed., *A Little Book on the Human Shadow* (San Francisco: Harper & Row, 1988), 30–33.

15. Bly, "Five Stages in Exiling, Hunting, and Retrieving the Shadow," 29.

16. Carol Rittner, "An Interview with Elie Wiesel," *America* 159, no. 15 (Nov. 19, 1988): 404.

17. Octavio Paz, *One Earth, Four or Five Worlds* (San Diego: Harcourt Brace Jovanovich, 1985).

18. Norman Mailer, "The White Negro," *Dissent*, 4 (Summer 1957), 276–293.

Chapter Nine. Plebeian Postmodernism

1. Bonhoeffer, *Letters and Papers from Prison*, 370.

2. Hannah Arendt, "Preface," *Between Past and Future* (New York: Viking, 1968), 14.

3. Spink, *Life in the Spirit*, 24–25.

4. Ocatavio Paz, *The Labyrinth of Solitude*, trans. Lysander Kemp (New York: Grove Press, 1961), 175.

5. Coretta King, *Words of Martin Luther King*, 17.

6. Solzhenitsyn, *The First Circle*, trans. Thomas P. Whitney (New York: Harper & Row, 1968), 389.

7. Eileen Egan, *Such a Vision of the Street* (Garden City, NY: Doubleday, 1985), 35.

8. Louis Valdez's screenplay *Zoot Suit*.

9. *Mother Teresa*, a film produced and directed by Ann Petrie and Jeanette Petrie.

10. Gandhi, *Collected Works*, vol. 17, 407.

11. Allen Ginsberg, *Allen Verbatim* (New York: McGraw-Hill, 1974), 30.

12. Jacques Ellul, *The Presence of the Kingdom*, trans. Olive Wyon (New York: Seabury Press, 1967), 56.

13. Roland Barthes, *The Pleasure of the Text*, trans. Richard Miller (New York: Hill & Wang, 1975), 30–31.

14. Bernard-Henri Levy, *The Testament of God*, trans. George Holock (New York: Harper & Row, 1979), xi.

15. Sanford Krolick, *Recollective Resolve* (Macon, Ga: Mercer University Press, 1987), 92–99.

16. Jerome Rothenberg and Diane Rothenberg, *The Symposium of the Whole* (Berkeley, CA: University of California Press, 1983), xi.

17. Nikolai Berdyaev, quoted by William D. Miller, *A Harsh and Dreadful Love* (New York: Liveright, 1973), 7.

18. Dagobert Runes, *Dictionary of Philosophy* (New York: Philosophical Library, 1960), 244.

19. Nouwen, *Reaching Out*, 54.

20. "Preface" to Ann and Jeanette Petrie's film *Mother Teresa*.

INDEX

Abernathy, Ralph
  on King
    *And the Walls Came Tumbling
    Down,* 85
Adorno, Theodore
  as critic of everyday life, 9
  Negative Dialectics, 10n.7
advaita
  as dehistoricized truth, 23
African-American Church
  as inspiration to King, 13
agape
  and King, 90
ahimsa
  and *The Great Tradition,* 27
  as wager and poetic, 24
  overcoming duality, 19
alienation
  not a plebeian theme, 12
Alyosha's kiss
  and the plebeian sublime, 74
Another Mother Tongue, 3n.2
Ansbro, John J.
  *Martin Luther King Jr.—The
  Making of a Mind,*
  90n.19
anti-intellectualism
  of Gandhi, 29
  of Mother Teresa, 115
  of Walesa, 115
antifoundationalism
  of Gandhi, 28
Apologia Pro Vita, 14
Apostle Paul
  as inspiration to King, 93
Arendt, Hannah
  Between Past and Future, 124n.2
  on thinking, 124

Aristotle
  poetics, 56
  politics, 130
Arnold, Matthew, 133
  Culture and Anarchy, 14
art
  and history, 45
  and holy madness in Wiesel, 56
  and ideas in the modern world,
    27
  and modernism, 11
  and moral virtue in Solzhenitsyn,
    45
  as constructive response to mod-
    ernist dilemmas, 5
  postmodern action art, 69
artificial intelligence, 10
asceticism
  of Gandhi, 21
assimilation, 121
  and "The Jewish Question," in
    Wiesel, 57
  as plebeian theme, 12
  Jewish resistance to, in Wiesel, 60
  problematics of, 136, 137
Attenborough, Richard
  Gandhi the film, 22
Auschwitz
  and sanity in Wiesel, 56
authority
  and spiritual witness, 43
Avant-garde
  contrasted to the plebeian
    postmodern, 37

Babbit, Sinclair Lewis, 117n.12
bad faith
  in everyday life, 9